1ST GRADE PHONICS
Unit 2
Uppercase Letters

MW01593373

TABLE OF CONTENTS

IMPORTANT: Please refer to the Teacher Guide for specific scripts, procedures, and words that are represented by pictures.

Throughout this Unit, learners will scan QR codes. Be careful they scan each code individually.

LEARN

- Alphabetical order
- Rhyming words
- Open and VCe syllables

VOCABULARY

alphabetical order
base word
suffix

open syllable
VCe syllable

DAILY PAGE GOALS

Day	Complete	Day	Complete	Day	Complete
1	ii–6	7	31–38	13	71–77
2	7–14	8	39–46	14	78–79
3	15–22	9	47–53	15	80–86
4	23–26	10	54–59	16	87–90
5	27–28	11	60–61	17	91–92
6	29–30	12	62–70	18	93–94

Teacher reads all pages to the Learners.

1. WHAT IS THE ALPHABET?

Learn:

- Listen to the ABC song.
- Read words with suffix **s**.

Vocabulary:

alphabetical order *[ăl fĭ ´bě tĭ kŭl ´or der]* – the order of letters in the alphabet

base word *[bās wĕrd]* – the shortest form of a word

suffix *[´sŭ fĭks]* – one or more letters added to the end of a base word

---

Listen and review.
Mark ⊠ when done.

1

THE ALPHABET

You have learned all the letters in the alphabet! Now you will learn about alphabetical order. **Alphabetical order** is the order of letters in the alphabet. We call it ABC order for short.

The ABC song will help you.

Listen to the song. Point to the letters as you hear them.

a b c d e f g h i

j k l m n o p q r

s t u v w x y z

WORKING WITH WORDS

A **base word** is the shortest form of a word. It makes sense by itself.

jet   van   disc

A **suffix** is one or more letters added to the end of a base word. Suffix **s** can change a base word to mean two or more things.

jet**s**   van**s**   disc**s**

Reading Rules

Suffix **s**: Suffix **s** is voiced after a voiced sound. It is unvoiced after an unvoiced sound.

dogs

cats

voiced

unvoiced

Write and circle.
Write each word with suffix **s**.
Then, circle if suffix **s** is voiced or unvoiced.

1) sled _____ voiced   unvoiced

2) mint _____ voiced   unvoiced

3) lip _____ voiced   unvoiced

4) pal _____ voiced   unvoiced

5) spot _____ voiced   unvoiced

WRITING PHONOGRAM REVIEW

Listen to and write the phonograms.
Underline any multi-letter phonograms.

SCORE   CORRECT   RESCORE

ACTIVITY: Suffix s

Circle the suffixes. Write the base words.

hips

_____

hens

_____

logs

_____

slugs

_____

cliffs

_____

cubs

_____

ants

_____

crabs

_____

fans

_____

hats

_____

2. WHAT ARE THE UPPERCASE LETTERS FOR *a*, *b*, AND *c*?

Learn:

- Write the uppercase letters for **a**, **b**, and **c**.

- Read sentences.

UPPERCASE LETTERS

In this Unit, you will learn uppercase letters. All uppercase letters are tall. We use them at the beginning of names and sentences. Then, we call them capital letters.

**Listen and review.
Mark ☒ when done.**

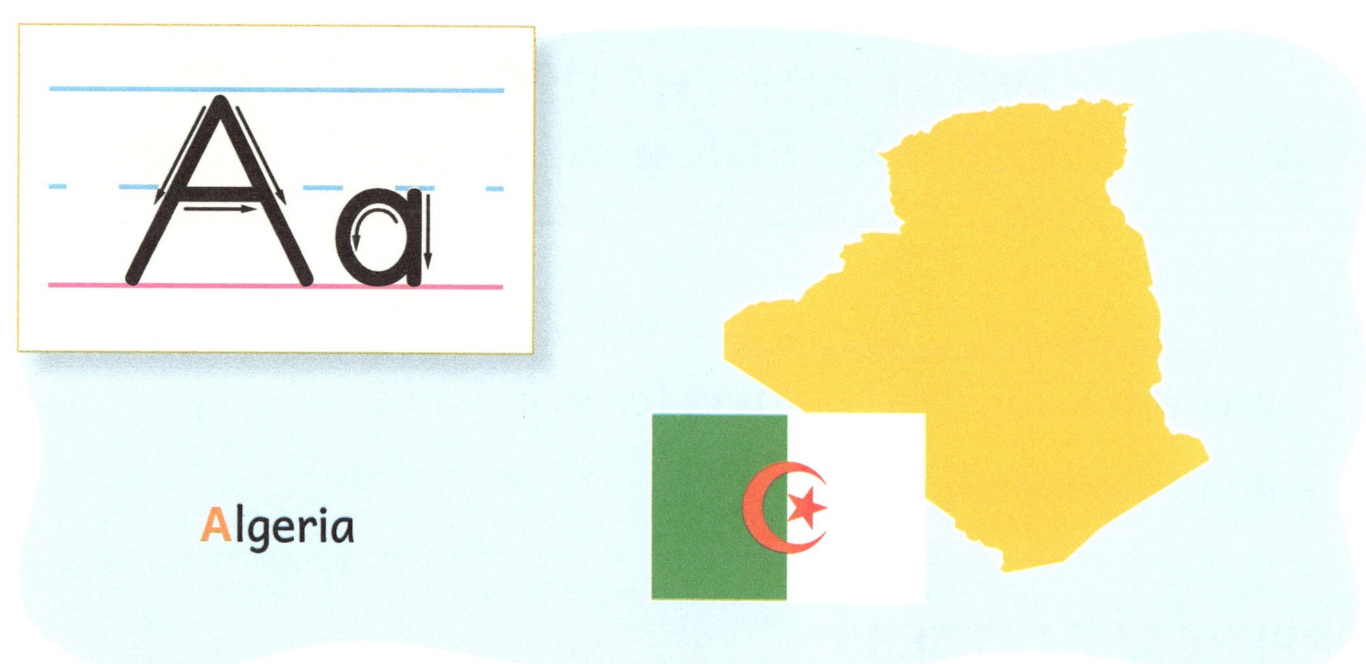

Algeria

 **Trace and write the letters.**

Write the names.

1) Al   2) Ann   3) Ax

Brazil

 **Trace and write the letters.**

Write the names.

4) Brad   5) Bob   6) Bess

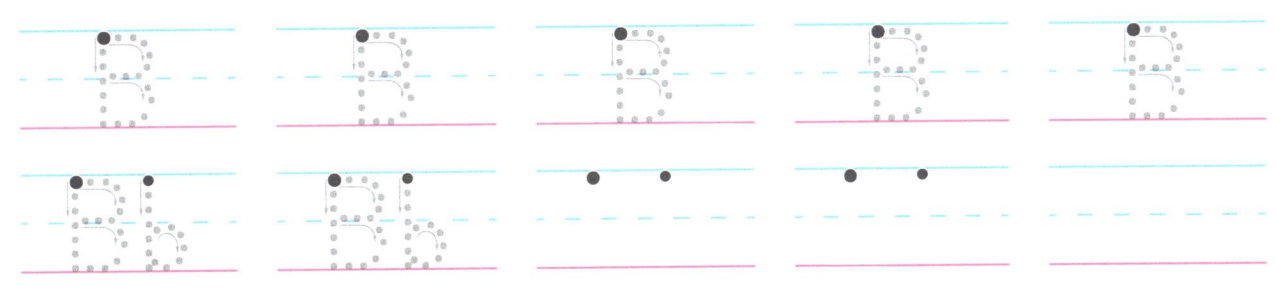

9

Cuba

Trace and write the letters.

C C C C C

Cc Cc

Write the names.

7) Cal   8) Cam   9) Cass

 **Write the missing capital letters.**

10) _____ , **B** , _____

WORKING WITH WORDS

Sentences begin with a capital letter. They end with a punctuation mark.

Most sentences end with a period. It is a dot. It means the sentence is telling something. Read the words calmly.

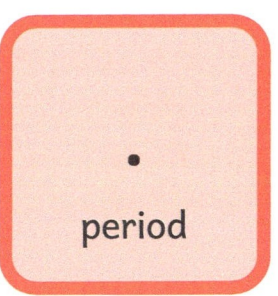

period

capital letter   period

Ben sits in class.

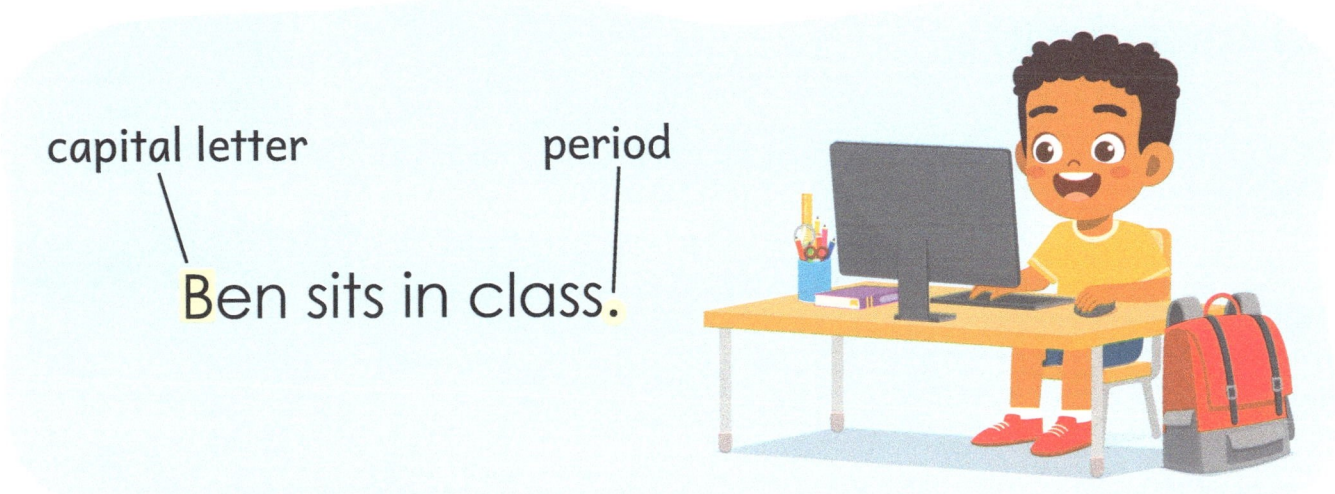

 **Match the sentences with the pictures.**

11) Bugs can hop.

12) Cats can nap.

13) Ants can lift.

WRITING PHONOGRAM REVIEW

Listen to and write the phonograms.
Underline any multi-letter phonograms.

SCORE   CORRECT   RESCORE

ACTIVITY: Color by Letter

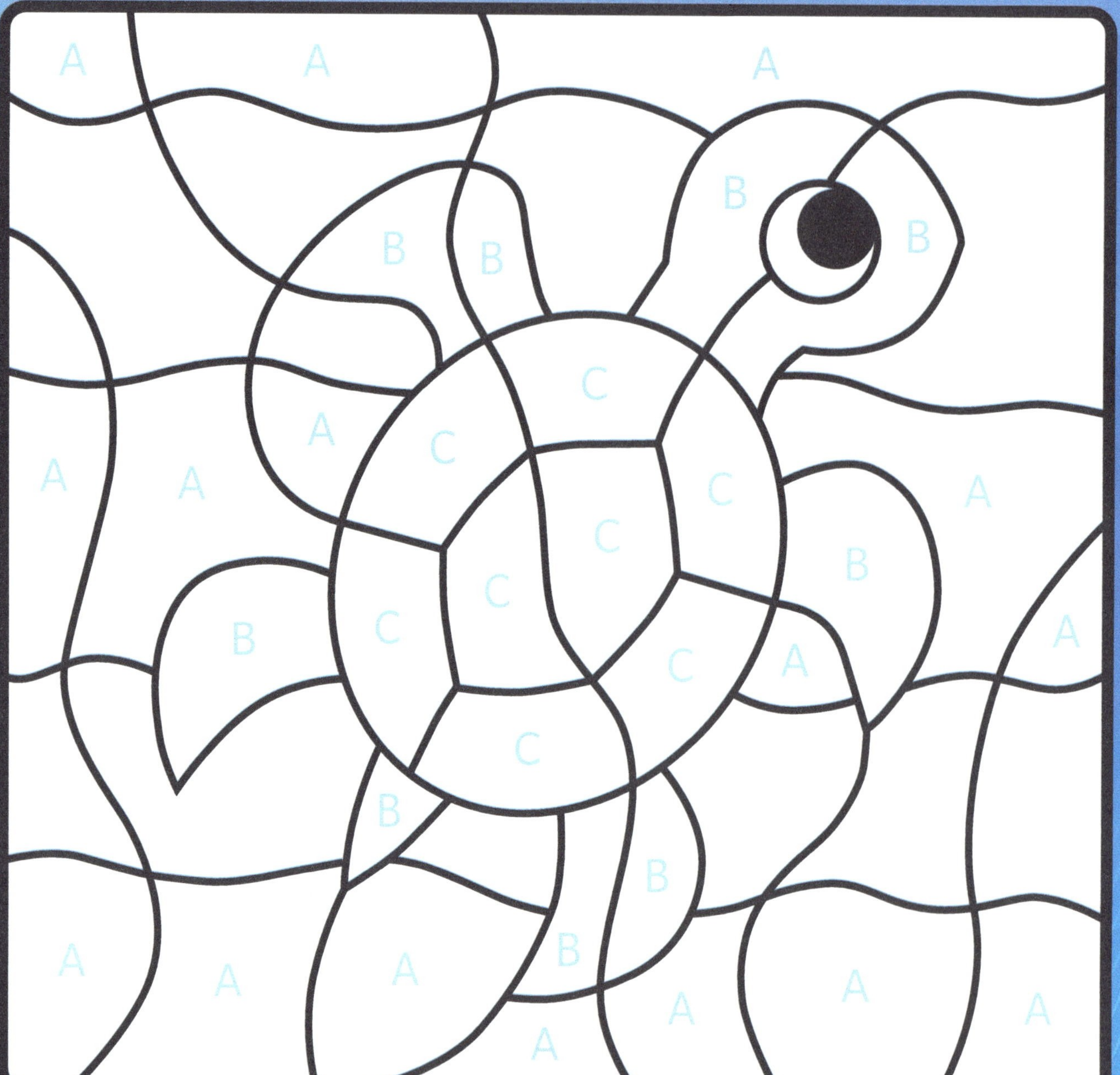

A A A

B B B B

C
A C
A A C C A
B C C B
C A A
B

B B
A A A A A
A

Color Key

A = blue   B = green   C = brown

3. WHAT ARE THE UPPERCASE LETTERS FOR d, e, f, AND g?

Learn:

- Write the uppercase letters for **d**, **e**, **f**, and **g**.
- Read open syllables.

Vocabulary:

open syllable [́ō pĕn ́sĭ lŭ bŭl] – a syllable with one vowel at the end that makes its long sound

---

**Listen and review.
Mark ☒ when done.**

15

Denmark

Trace and write the letters.

D   D   D   D   D

Dd   Dd

Write the names.

1) Dan   2) Deb   3) Dez

16

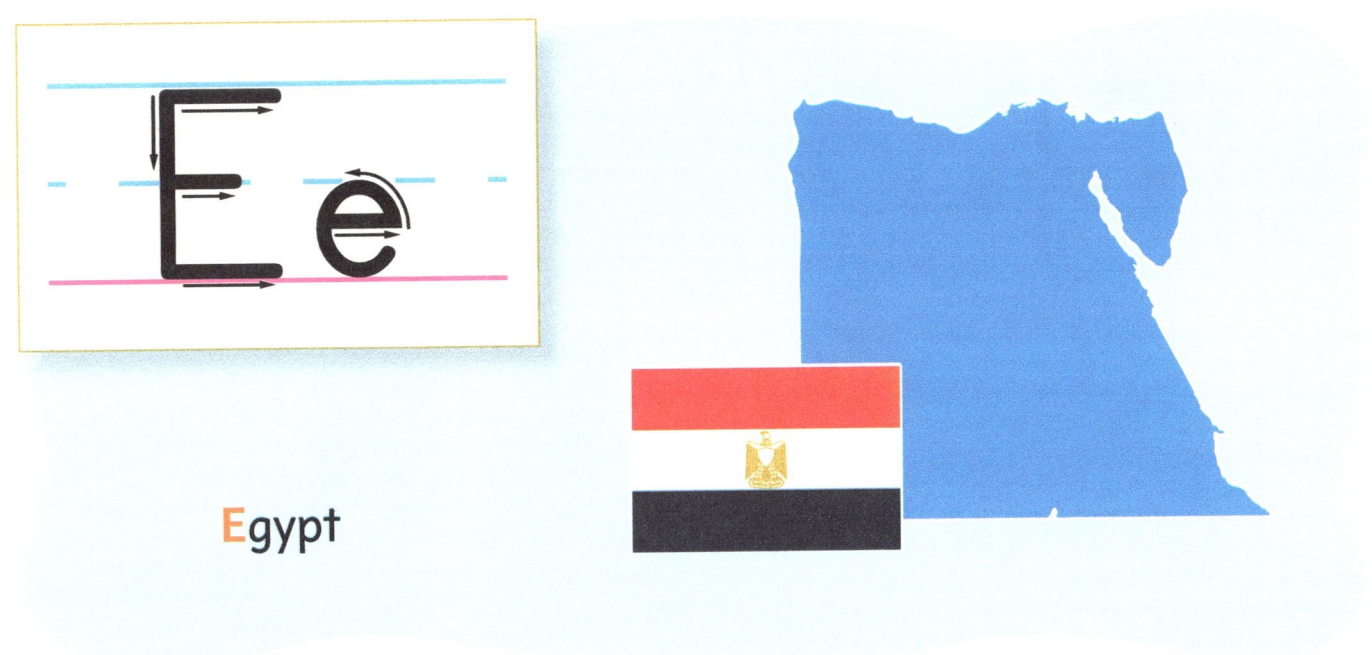

Egypt

Trace and write the letters.

Write the names.

4) Ed

5) Ell

6) Em

F f

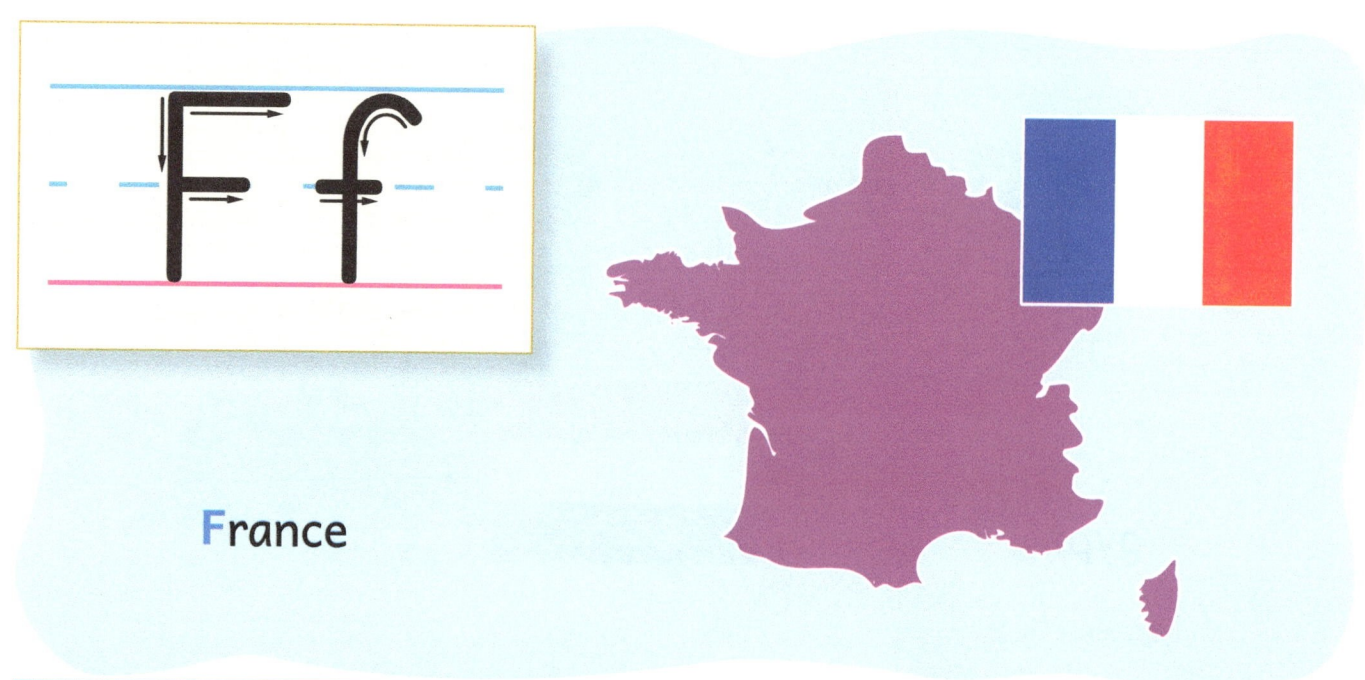

France

Trace and write the letters.

F F F F F

F f F f

Write the names.

7) Finn

8) Fran

9) Fitz

Germany

Trace and write the letters.

G G G G G

G g

Write the names.

10) Gus   11) Gwen   12) Glen

 **Write the missing capital letters.**

13) _____ , _____ , C , D , _____

WORKING WITH WORDS

Reading Rules

Open Syllables: An **open syllable** has one vowel letter. The vowel is at the end of the syllable and makes its long sound.

b **e**

a

p r **o**

Read, write, and circle the correct answers.

Read	Write	Circle

14) he

15) hi

16) no

17) we

18) me

WRITING PHONOGRAM REVIEW

Listen to and write the phonograms.
Underline any multi-letter phonograms.

SCORE   CORRECT   RESCORE

PHONOGRAM REVIEW

 Listen to and circle the correct phonograms.

1)    j   w   qu

2)    n   v   r

3)    g   y   p

4)    t   l   h

5)    y   o   j

23

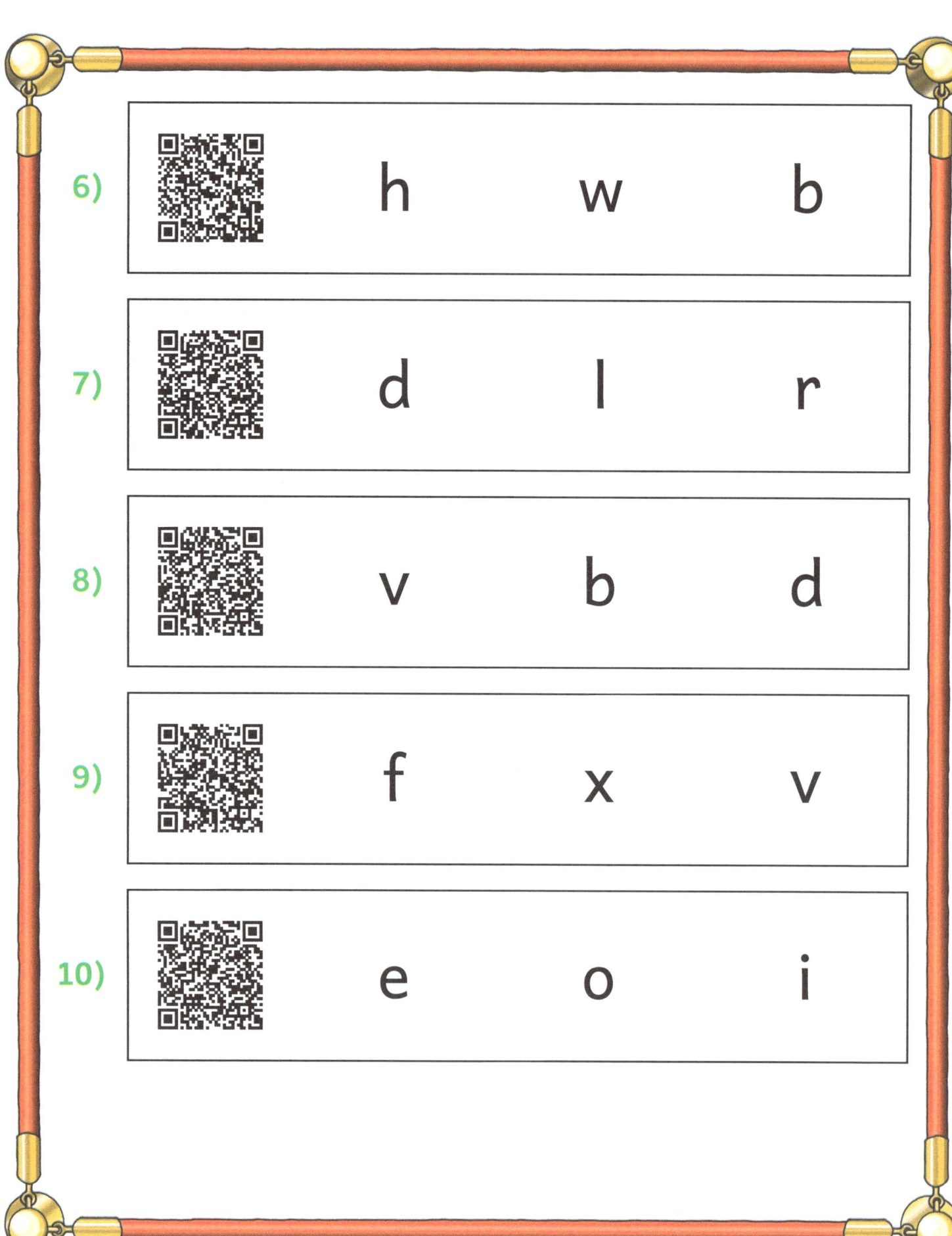

6)   h   w   b

7)   d   l   r

8)   v   b   d

9)   f   x   v

10)   e   o   i

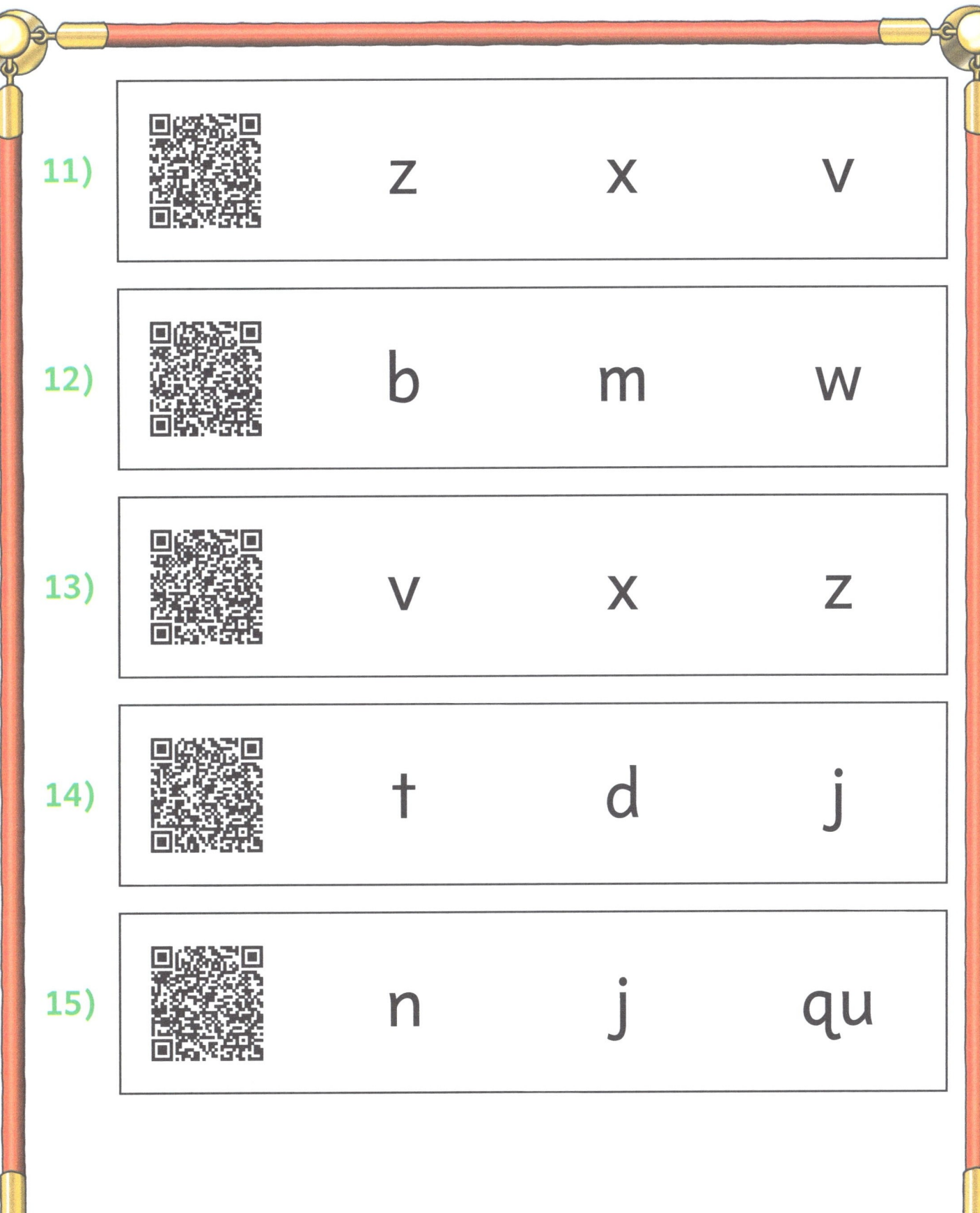

11) z   x   v

12) b   m   w

13) v   x   z

14) t   d   j

15) n   j   qu

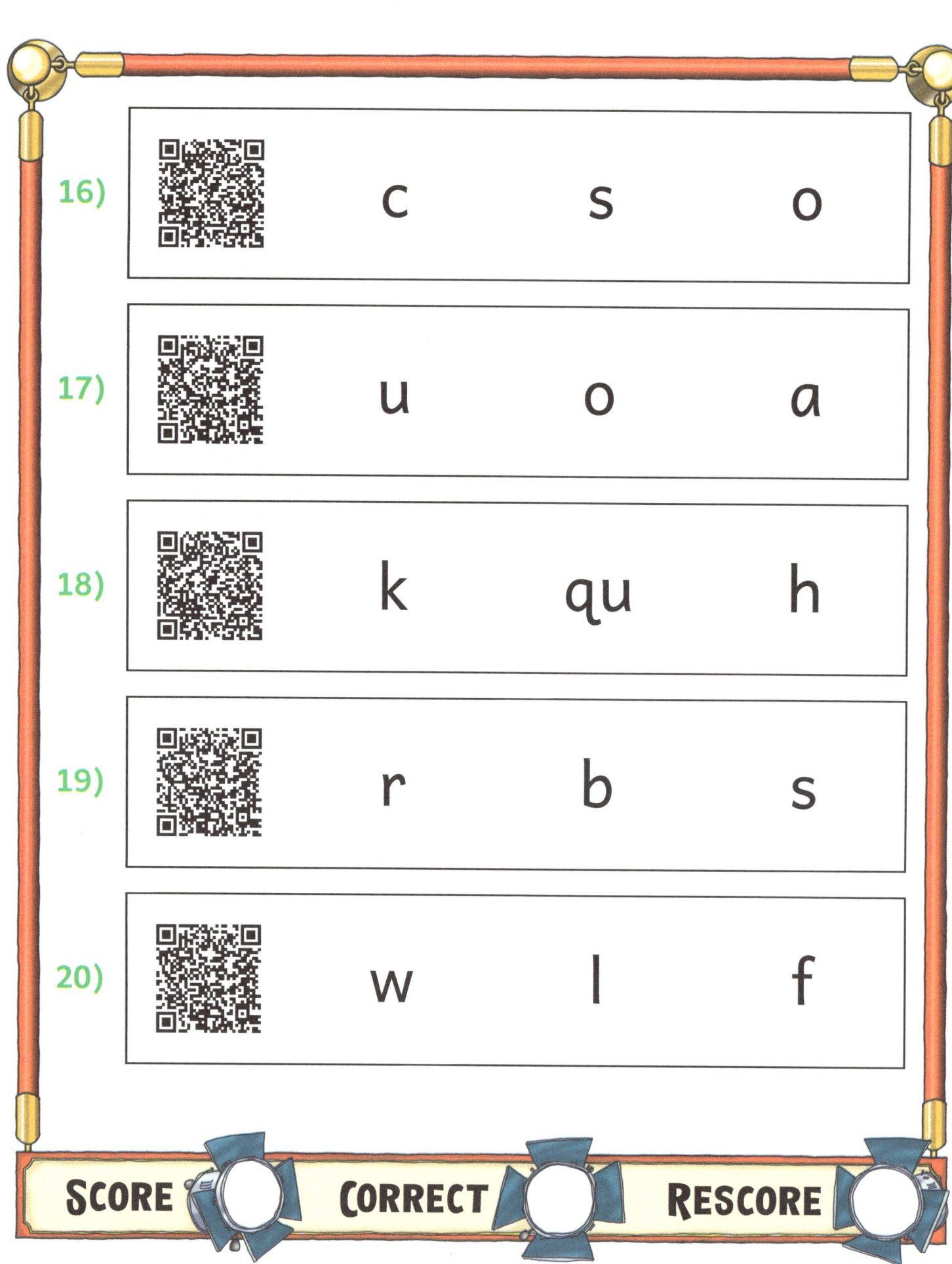

16) c   s   o

17) u   o   a

18) k   qu   h

19) r   b   s

20) w   l   f

SCORE   CORRECT   RESCORE

ACTIVITY: Reading Rules

You have learned two types of syllables. They tell you if a vowel sound will be short or long.

Closed	**Open**

m**e**t	m**e**
short vowel	long vowel

Read each word and mark ☒ the syllable type.

	Closed	**Open**
sit	☒	☒
a	☒	☒
so	☒	☒

	Closed	Open
at		
not		
be		
Ben		
fro		
no		
frog		

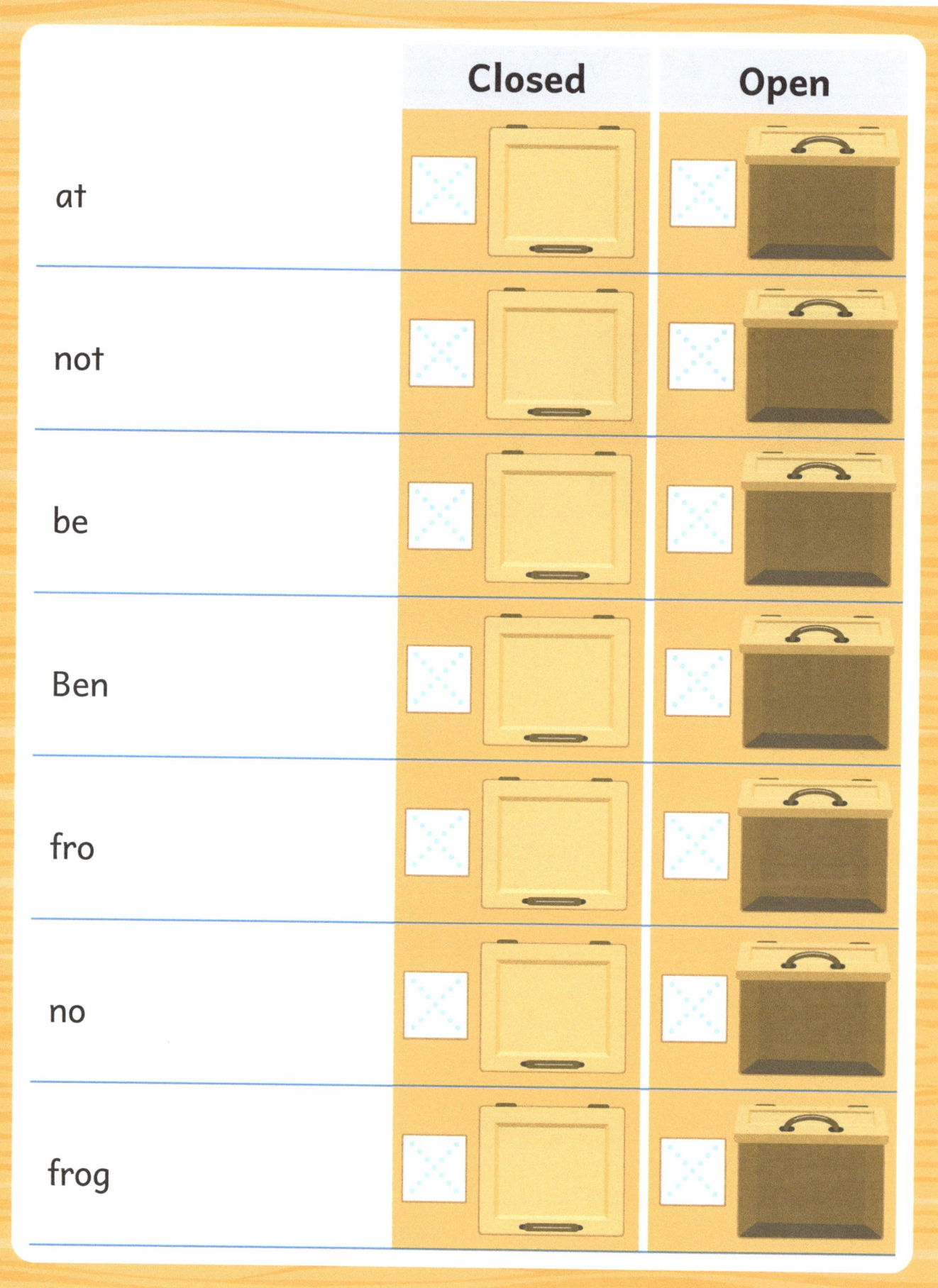

28

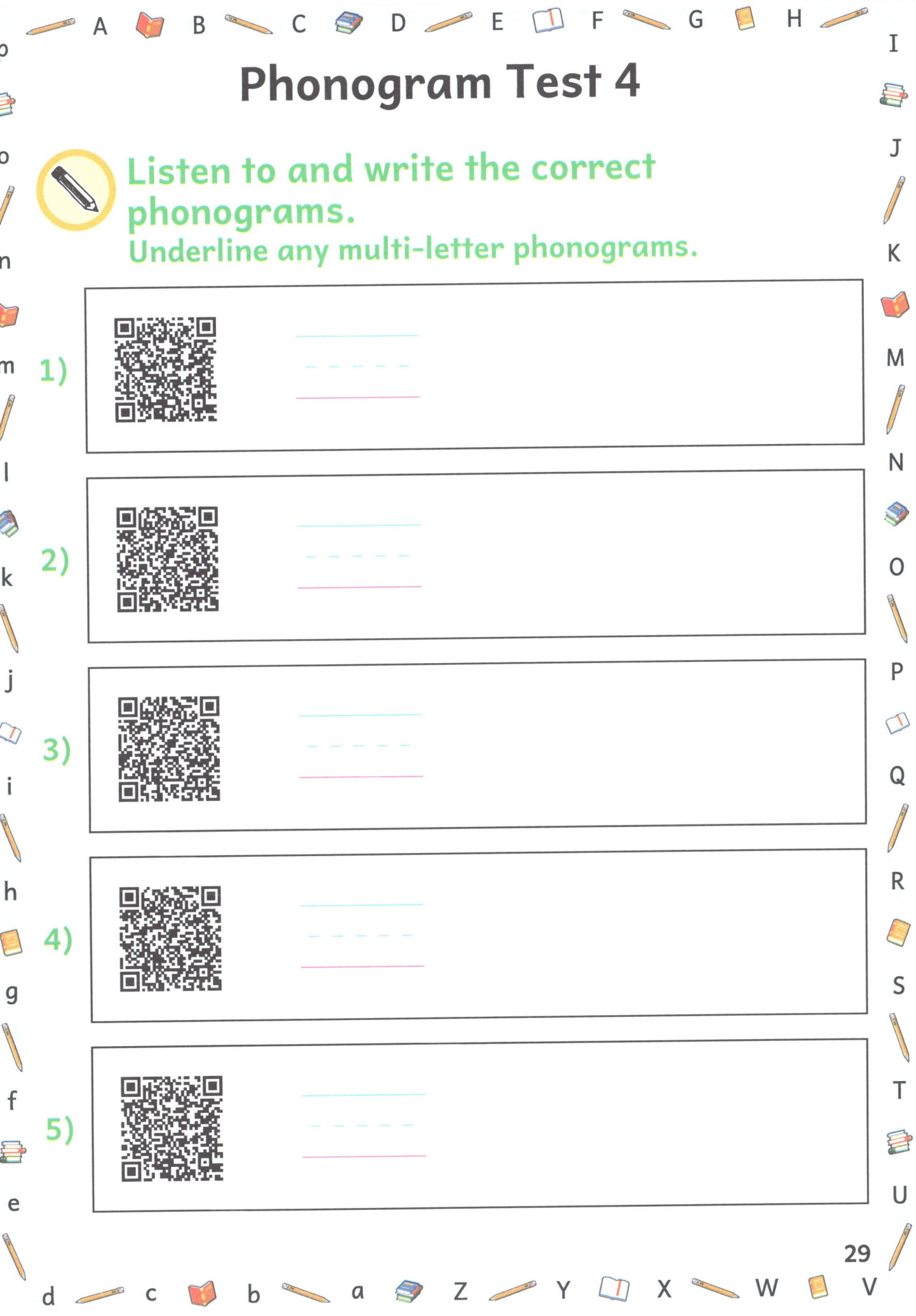

Phonogram Test 4

Listen to and write the correct phonograms.
Underline any multi-letter phonograms.

1)

2)

3)

4)

5)

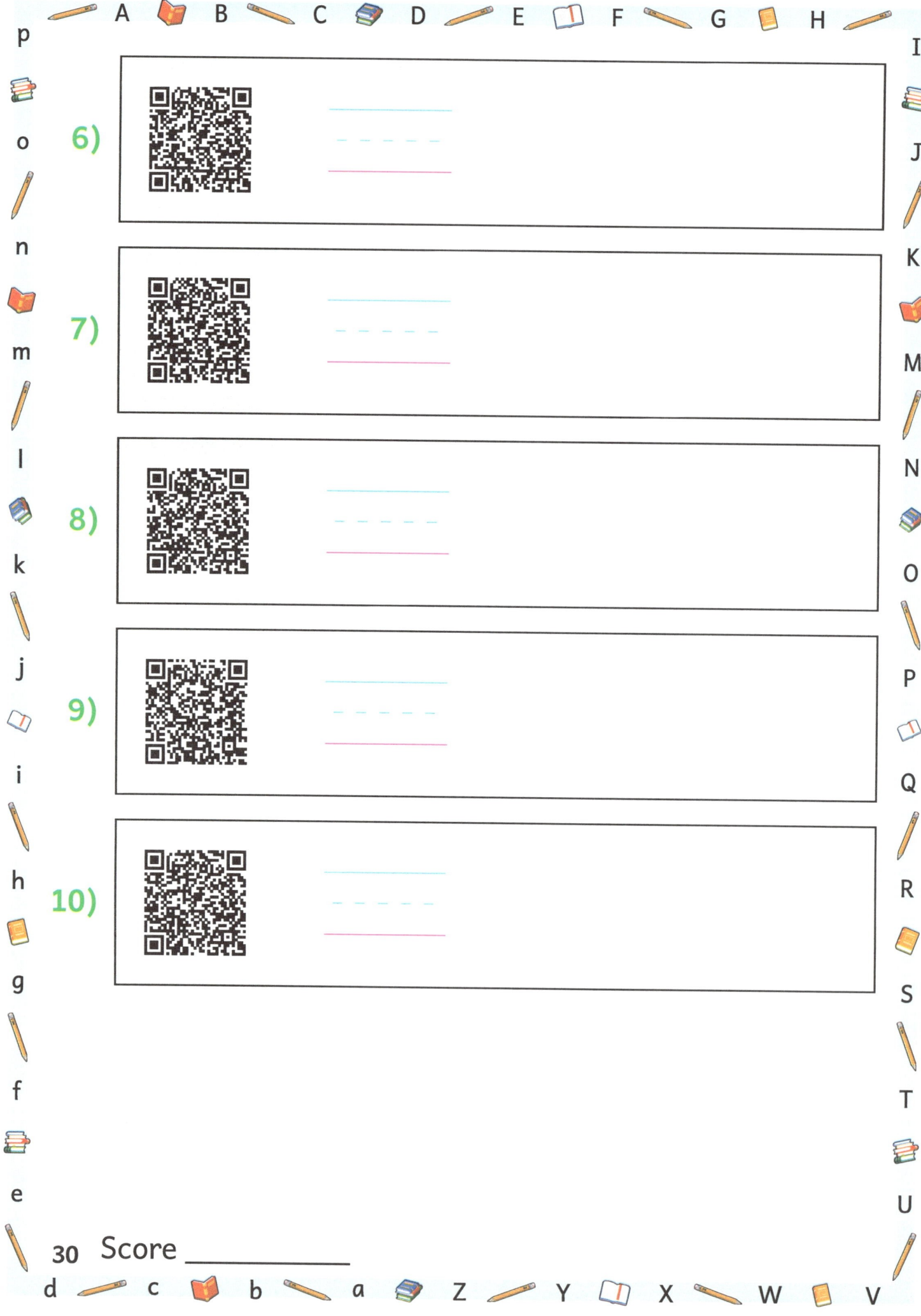

6)

7)

8)

9)

10)

Score _____

4. WHAT ARE THE UPPERCASE LETTERS FOR **h**, **i**, AND **j**?

Learn:

- Write the uppercase letters for **h**, **i**, and **j**.
- Read everyday words.

Listen and review.
Mark ☒ when done.

WORKING WITH SOUNDS

READING PHONOGRAM REVIEW

Haiti

🖊 **Trace and write the letters.**

Write the sentence.

1) Hal had a hot ham.

Italy

We use the word *I* to talk about ourselves. It is always capitalized.

Trace and write the letters.

Write the sentence.

2) He and I will sit in a bit.

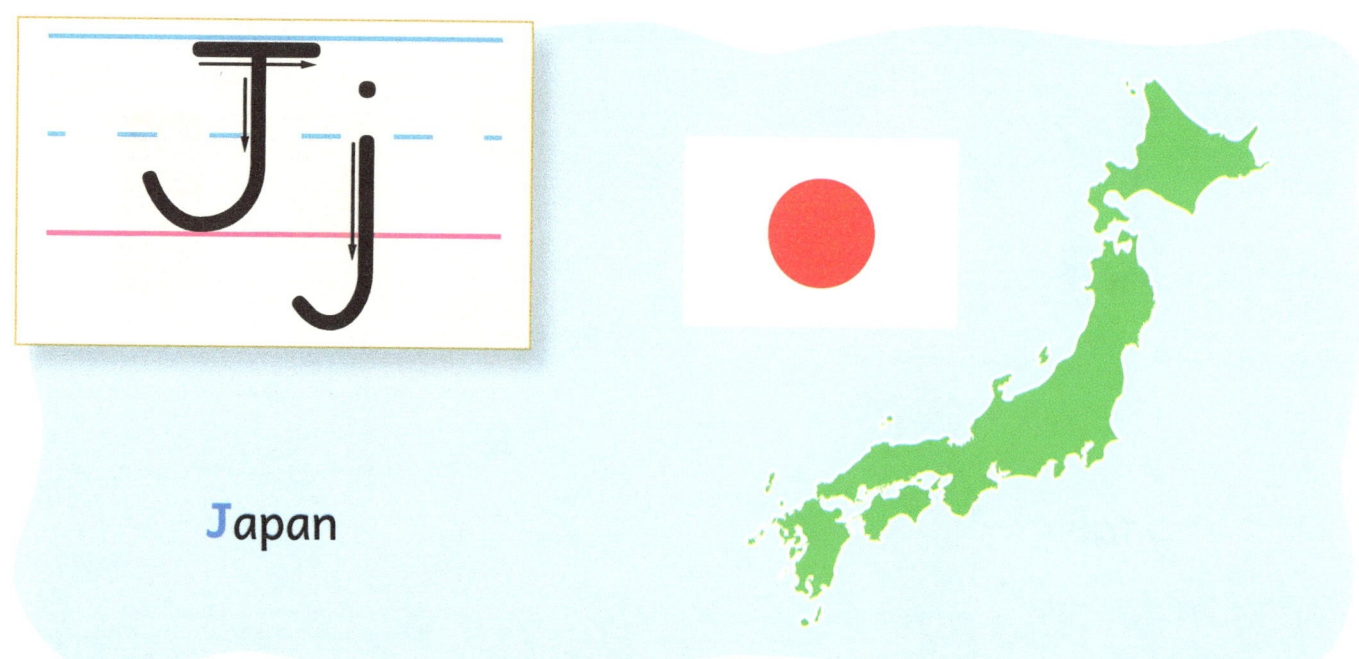

Japan

 **Trace and write the letters.**

Write the sentence.

3) Jill and I jump on a jet.

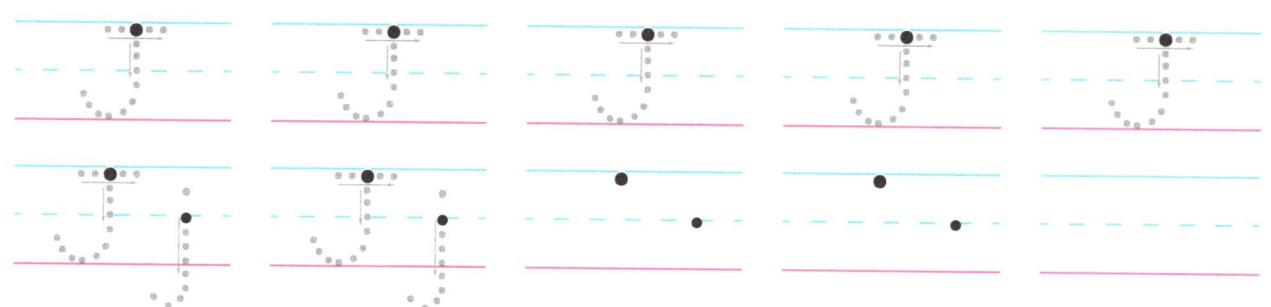

 **Write the missing capital letters.**

4) _____ , B , C , _____ , E , F , _____ ,

_____ , I , _____

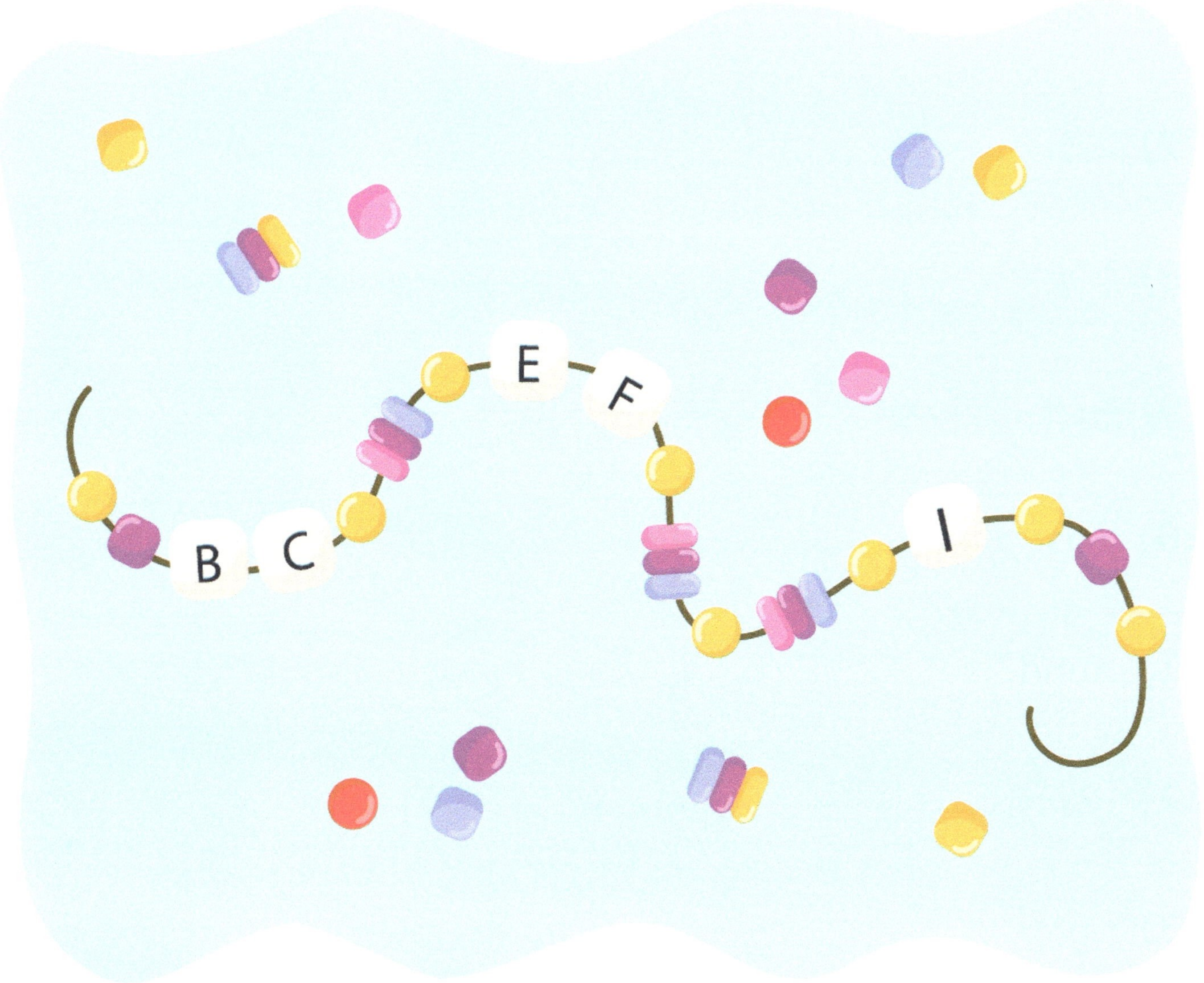

WORKING WITH WORDS

Everyday words are words that we use a lot. You will read and write them often. They have short and long vowels.

 # Read, trace, and write the everyday words.

Read	Trace	Write
5) a	a	
6) be	be	
7) if	if	
8) is	is	
9) so	so	
10) us	us	
11) and	and	
12) can	can	
13) got	got	
14) his	his	

WRITING PHONOGRAM REVIEW

Listen to and write the phonograms.
Underline any multi-letter phonograms.

SCORE   CORRECT   RESCORE

ACTIVITY: State Abbreviations

An abbreviation is a shortened word. In the United States, every state has its own abbreviation. It is two uppercase letters. It starts with the first letter of the state's name.

Abbreviation	State Name
ID	**Id**aho
GA	**G**eorgi**a**

Match the abbreviations to the state names.

CA	Hawaii
IA	Delaware
DE	California
HI	Iowa

5. WHAT ARE THE UPPERCASE LETTERS FOR **k**, **l**, **m**, AND **n**?

Learn:

- Write the uppercase letters for **k**, **l**, **m**, and **n**.

- Read tricky everyday words.

Listen and review.
Mark ☒ when done.

Kenya

Trace and write the letters.

Write the sentence.

1) Kim kept a kilt and a kit.

Lebanon

Trace and write the letters.

Write the sentence.

2) Liz lost a lid in a lab.

Mm

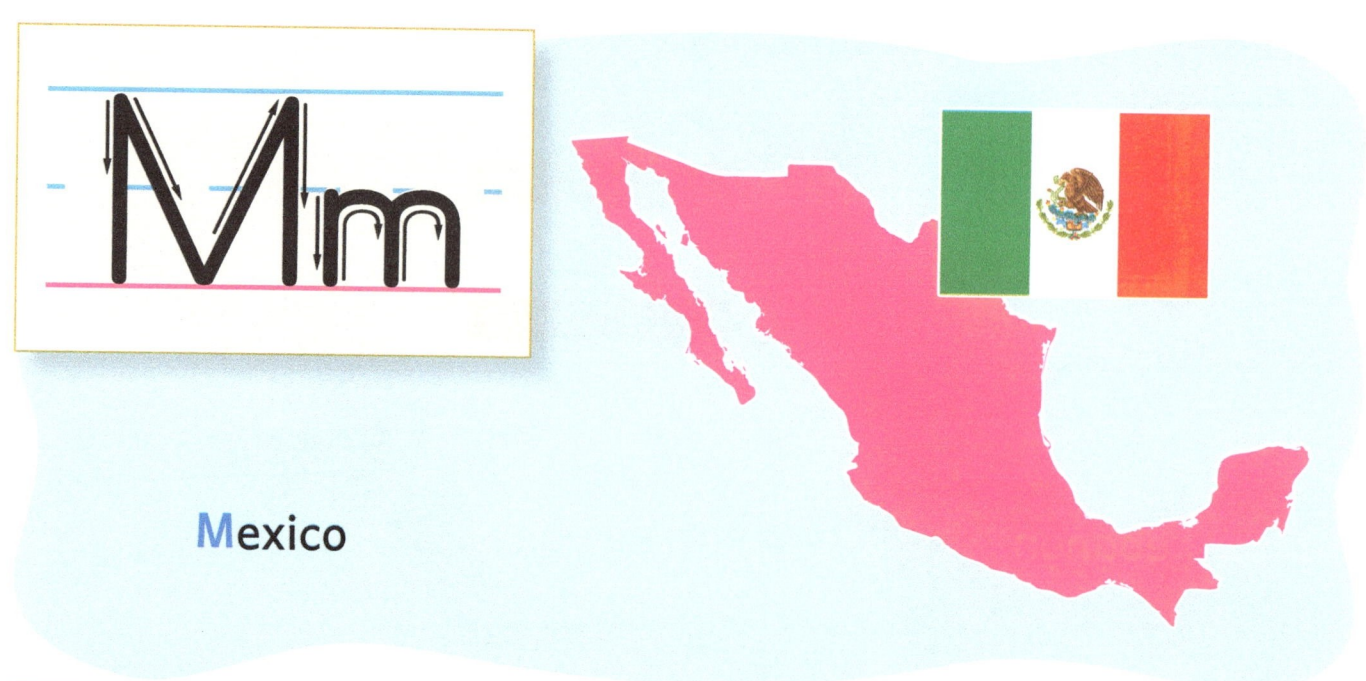

Mexico

Trace and write the letters.

Write the sentence.

3) Max got mud on a map.

Nepal

Trace and write the letters.

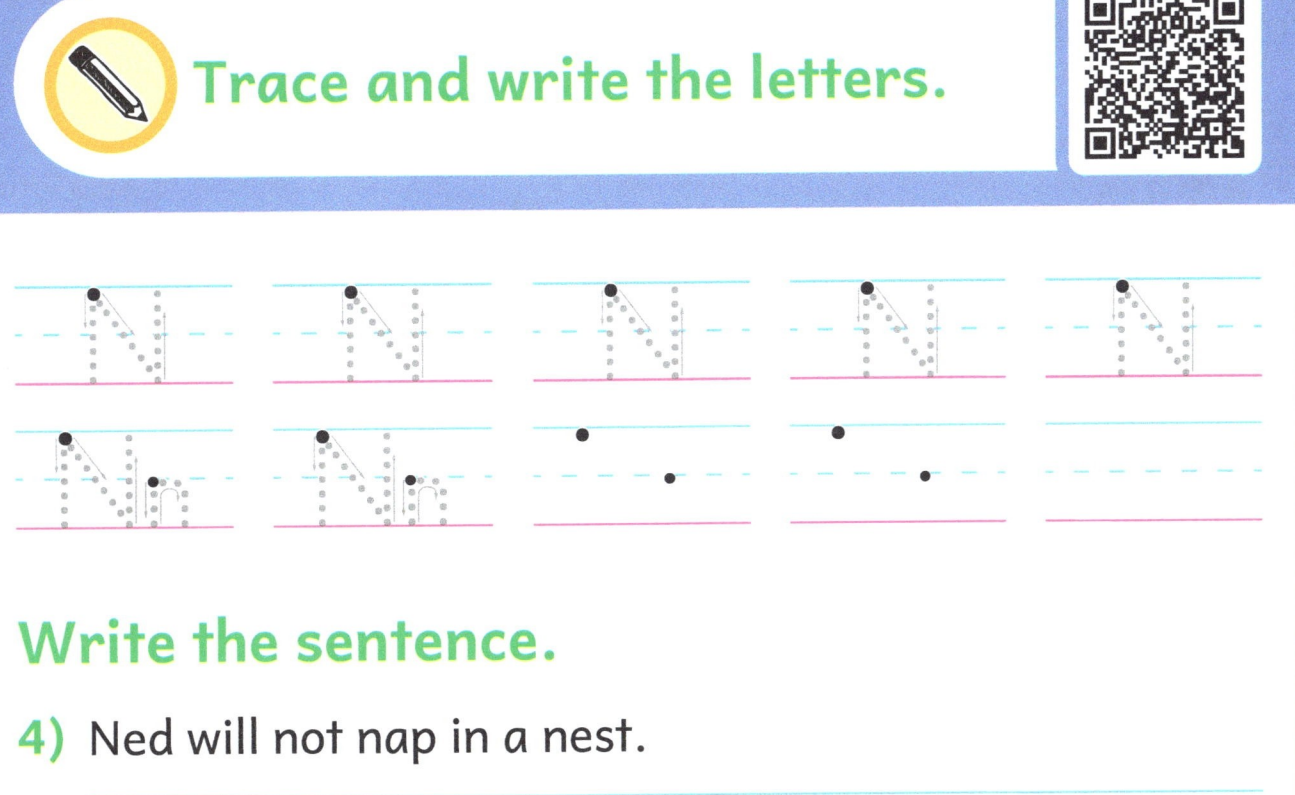

Write the sentence.

4) Ned will not nap in a nest.

 **Write the missing capital letters.**

5) A , B , ___ , D , E , ___ , G ,

H , ___ , J , K , ___ ,

WORKING WITH WORDS

These everyday words can be tricky. They have the third vowel sounds of **o**, **u**, and **a**.

 **Read, trace, and write the everyday words.**

Read	Trace	Write
6) do	do	
7) to	to	
8) put	put	
9) want	want	

Circle the correct answers.
Which picture describes the sentence?

10) I do not want to nap.

11) I put a bell on my cat.

12) I want to put on a mask and do a skit.

 **Listen to and write the phonograms.**
Underline any multi-letter phonograms.

SCORE · CORRECT · RESCORE

Learn:

- Write the uppercase letters for **o**, **p**, and **q**.

- Read words that end with the letter **y**.

Listen and review.
Mark ☒ when done.

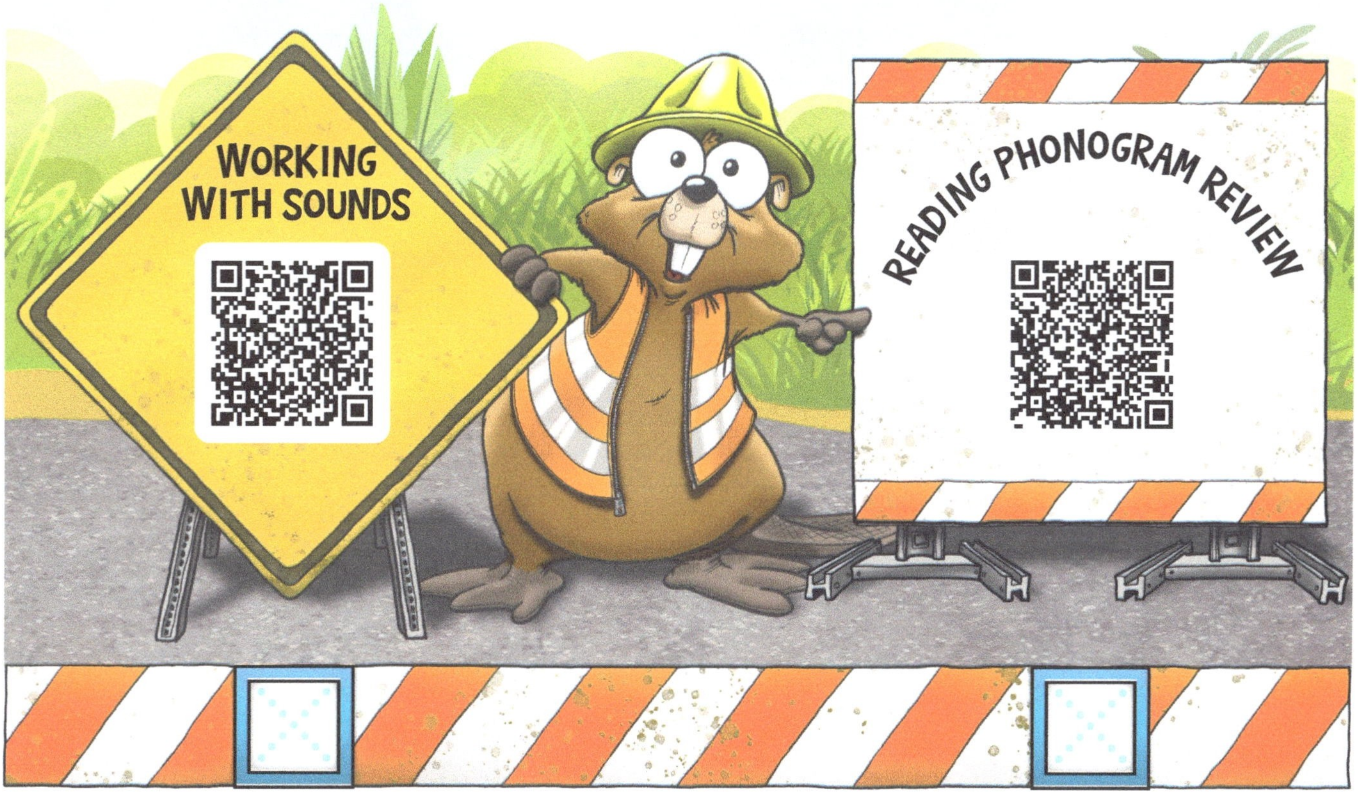

WORKING WITH SOUNDS

READING PHONOGRAM REVIEW

OH

✏️ Trace and write the letters.

Write the sentence.

1) Oz got on an odd ox.

Pp

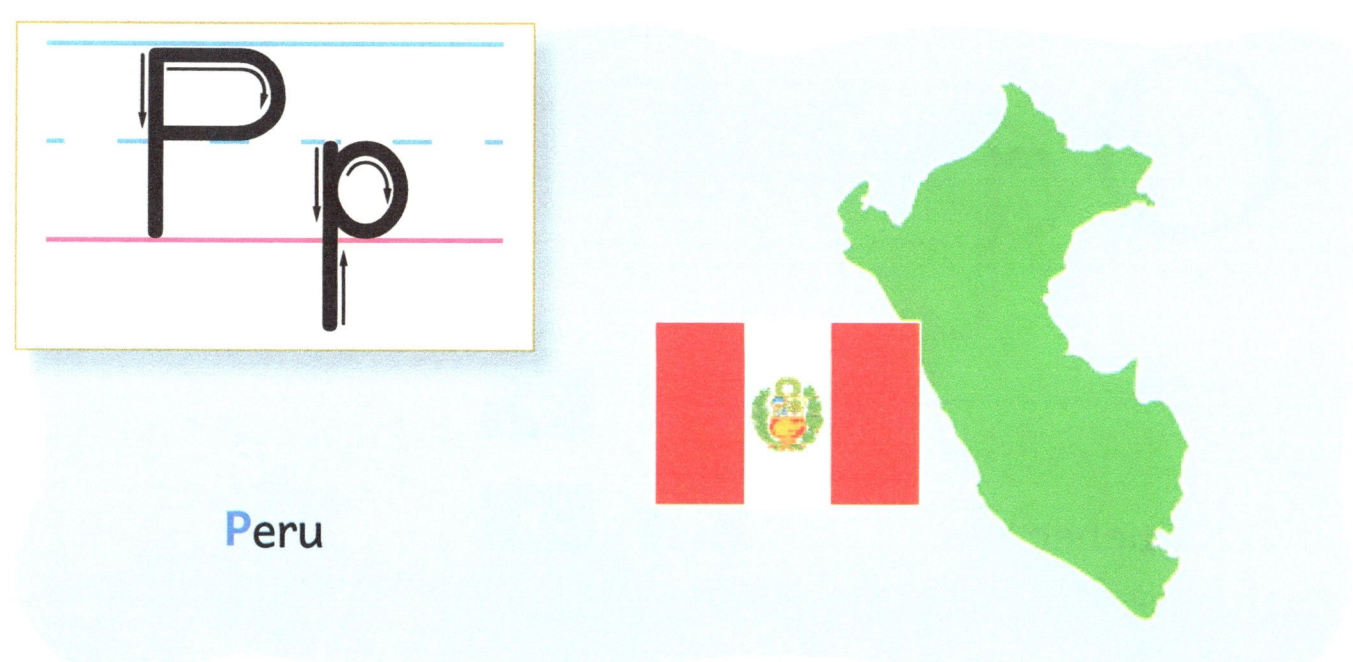

Peru

Trace and write the letters.

Write the sentence.

2) Pam had a pet pug.

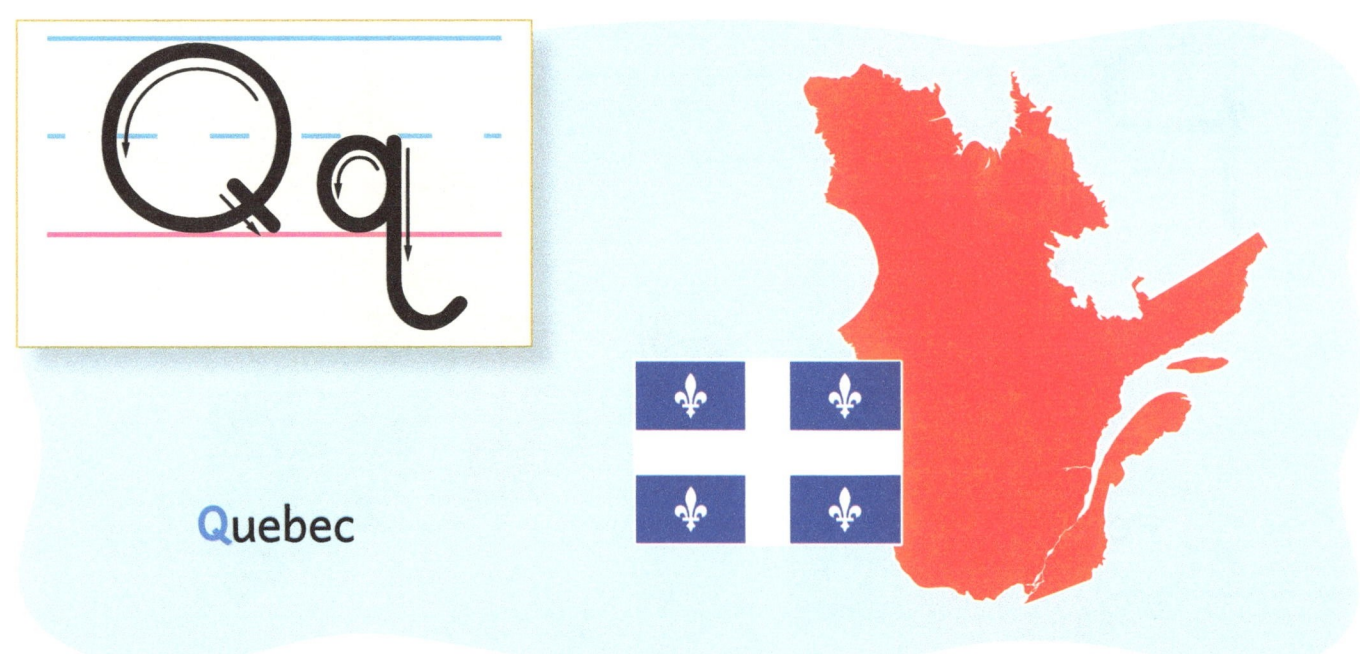

Quebec

Trace and write the letters.

Qq Qq Qq Qq Qq

Qq Qq

Write the sentence.

3) Quinn put a quill on a quilt.

Write the missing capital letters.

4) ___, ___, C, D, ___, F, ___,
H, ___, J, ___, ___, M, N,
___, P, ___

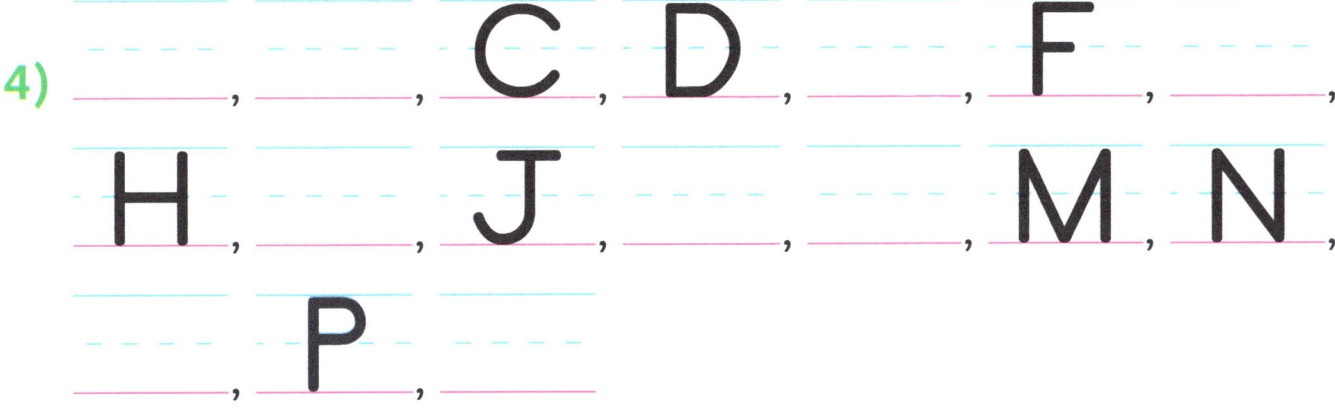

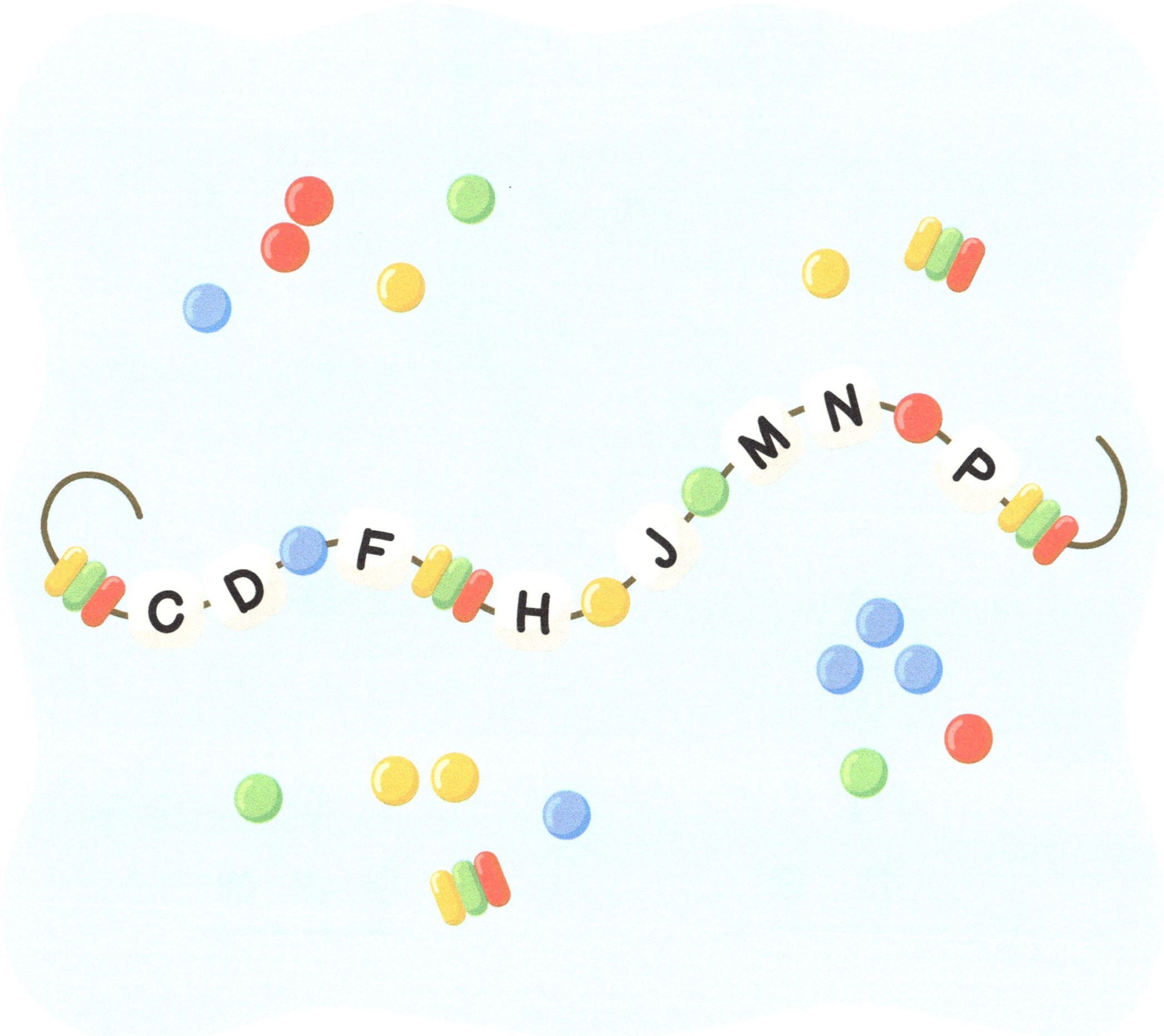

3rd Sound of **y**: The letter **y** makes its third sound at the end of a one-syllable word.

 **Circle the correct answers.**

5) Which sentence matches the picture?

I got a big fly.

My bats can fly.

6) Which sentence matches the picture?

I am a spy.

I sat by my cats.

7) Which sentence matches the picture?

Pam will try my jam.

Ken had a fry in a bag.

WRITING PHONOGRAM REVIEW

Listen to and write the phonograms.
Underline any multi-letter phonograms.

SCORE   CORRECT   RESCORE

PHONOGRAM REVIEW

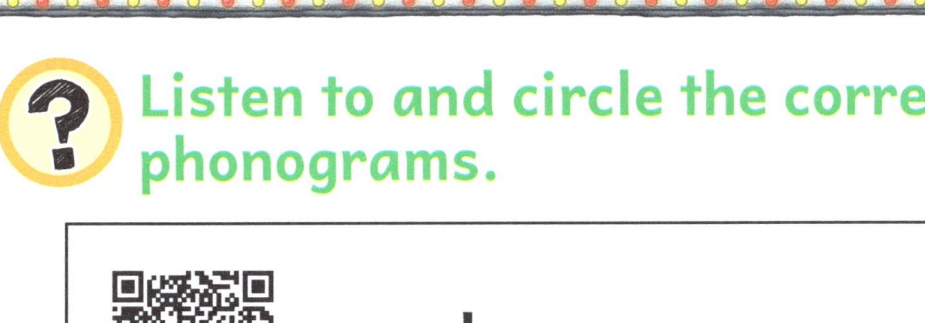

? Listen to and circle the correct phonograms.

1) k   x   z

2) w   r   a

3) s   c   d

4) o   a   i

5) e   o   u

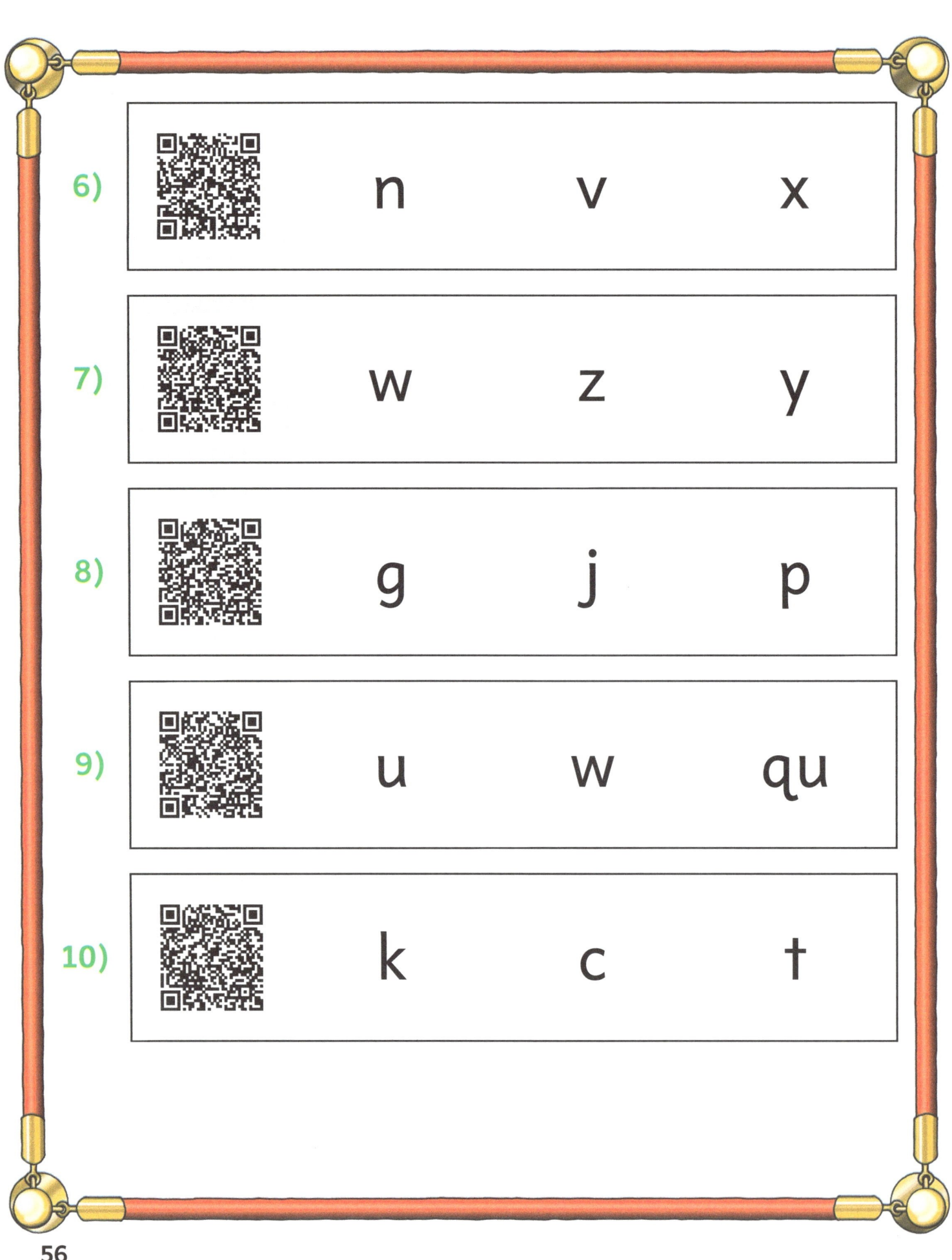

6)   n   v   x

7)   w   z   y

8)   g   j   p

9)   u   w   qu

10)   k   c   t

11) p h f

12) y i w

13) e s z

14) r n v

15) p qu j

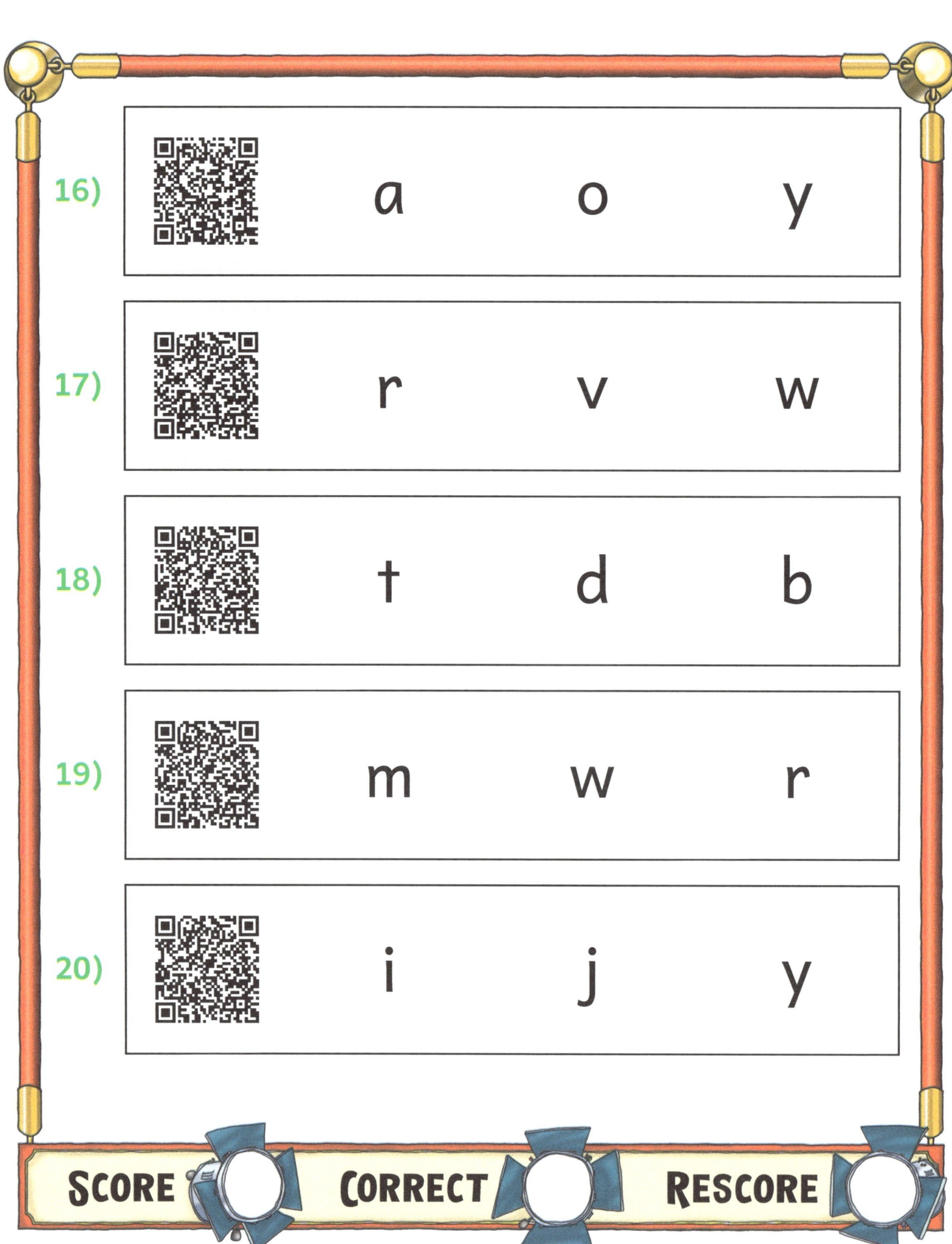

16)   a   o   y

17)   r   v   w

18)   t   d   b

19)   m   w   r

20)   i   j   y

SCORE   CORRECT   RESCORE

58

ACTIVITY: Rhyming Words

Complete the lists. Write two rhyming words.

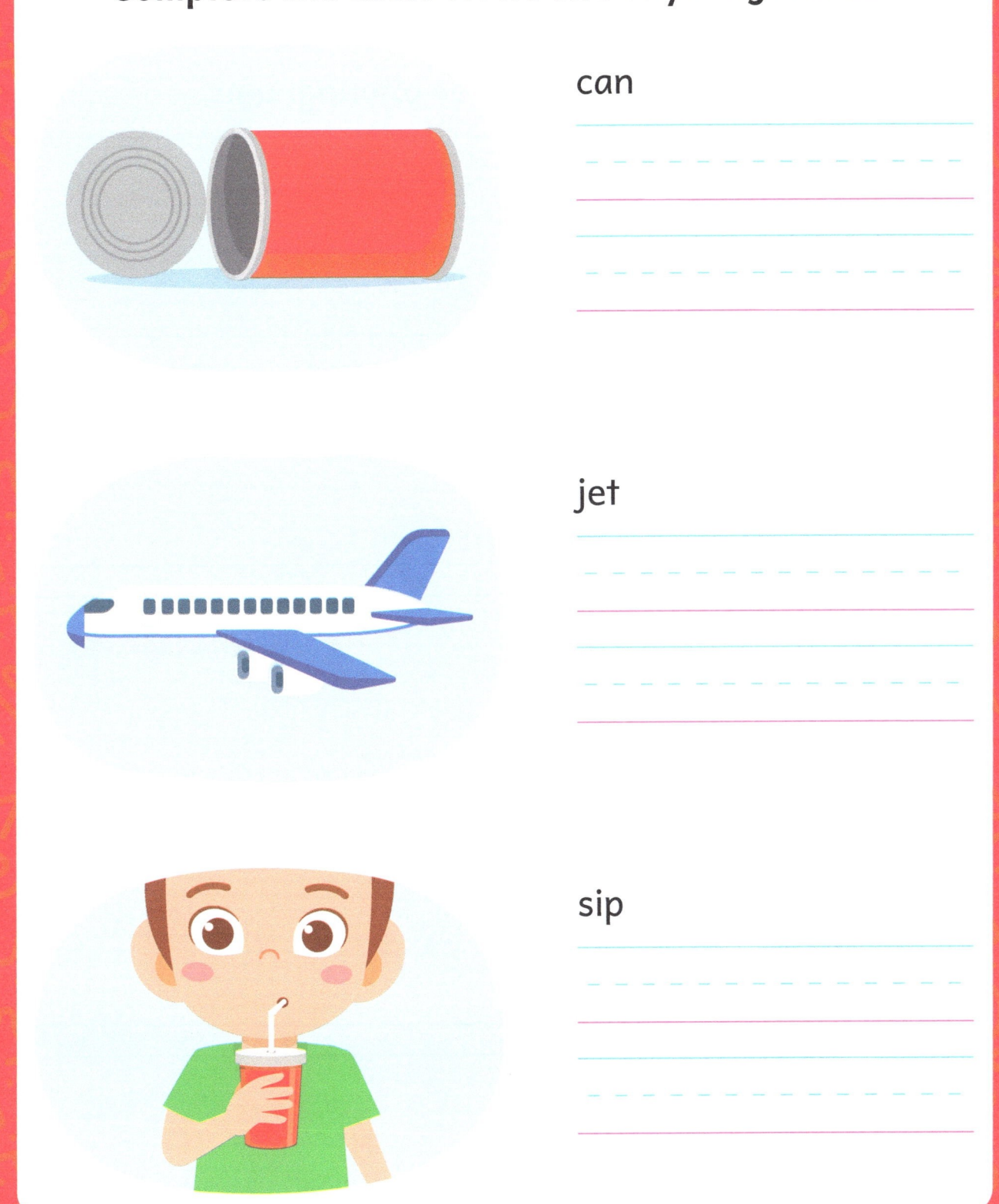

can
_____

jet
_____

sip
_____

Phonogram Test 5

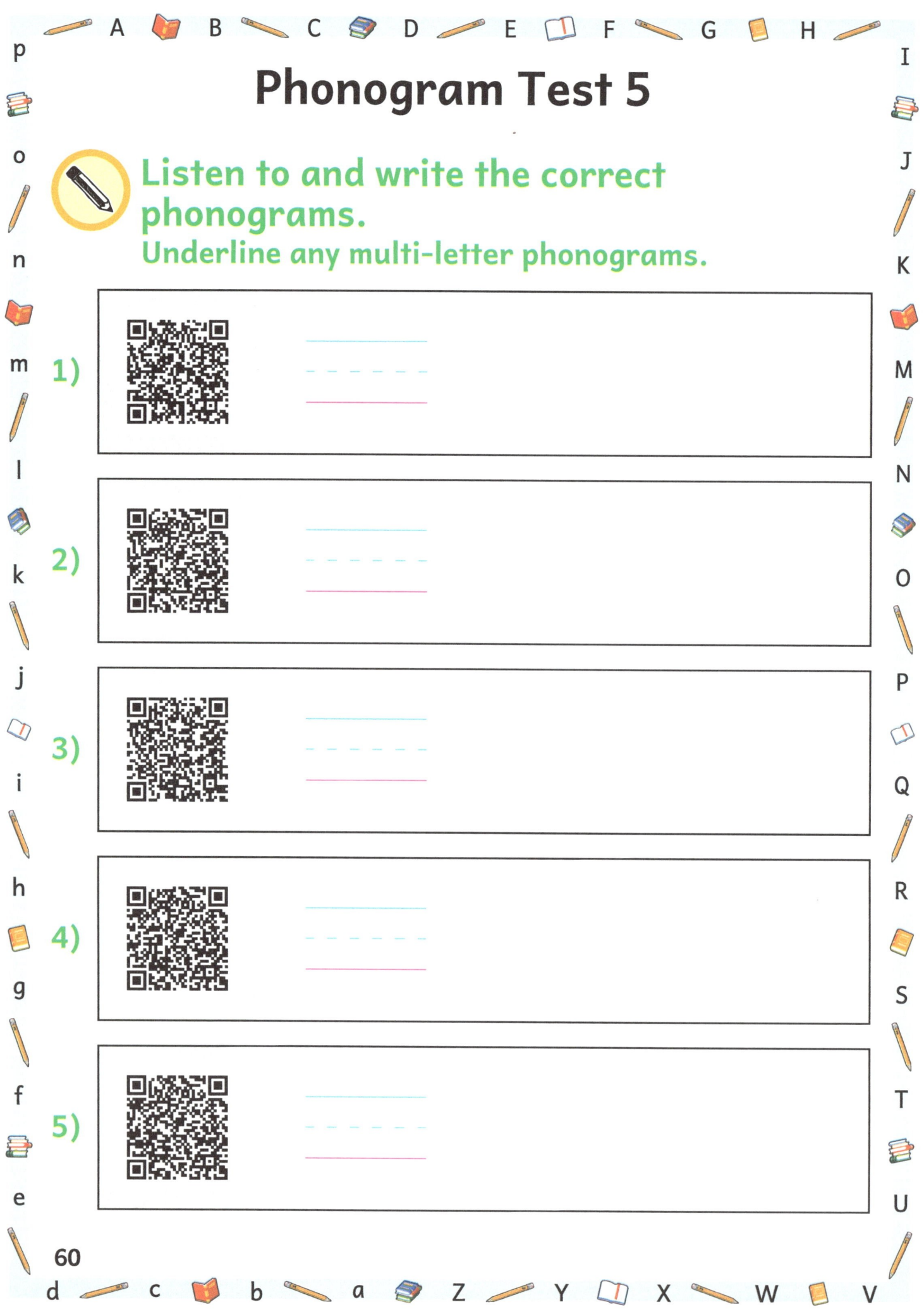

Listen to and write the correct phonograms.
Underline any multi-letter phonograms.

1)

2)

3)

4)

5)

60

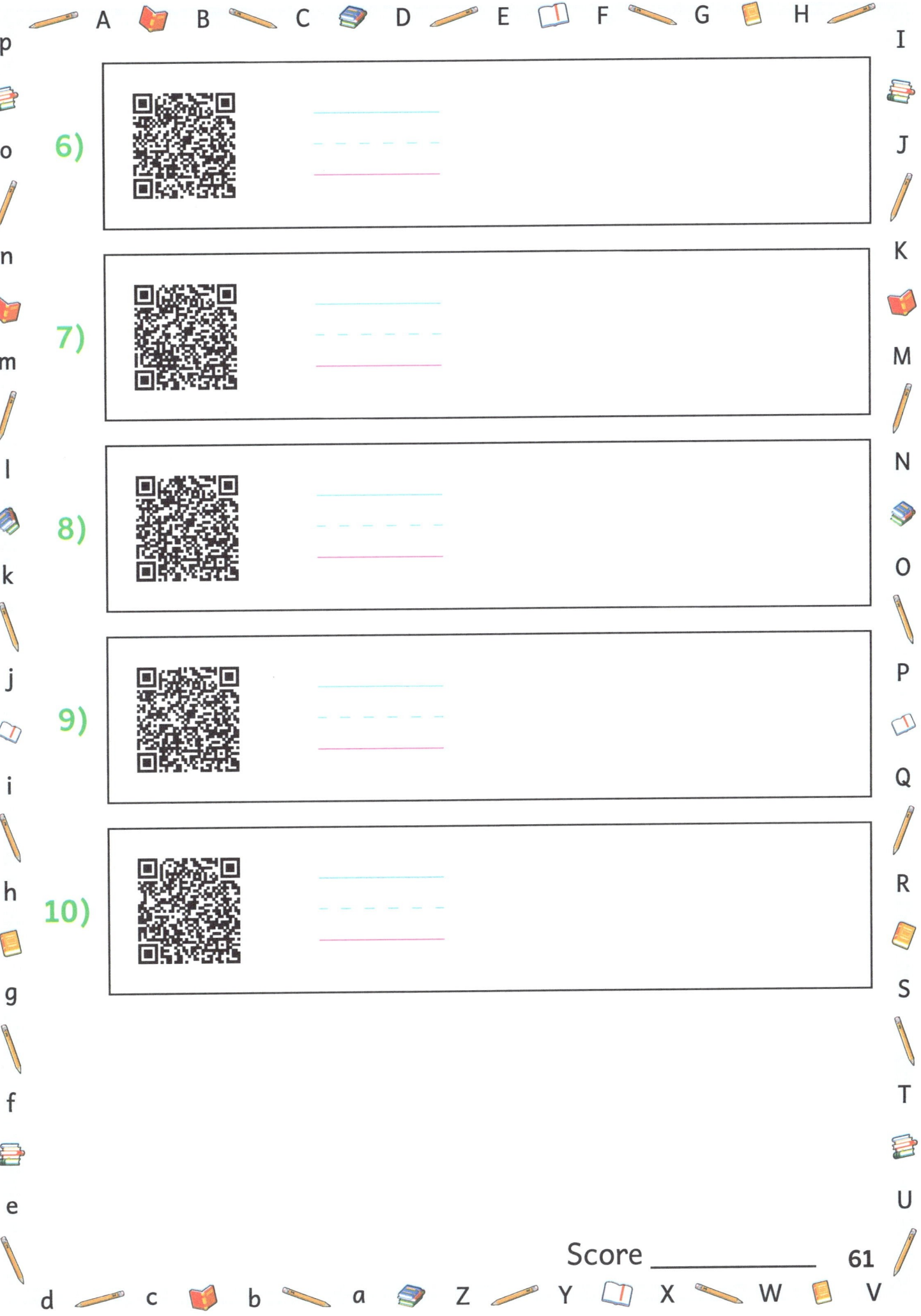

Score _____ **61**

7. WHAT ARE THE UPPERCASE LETTERS FOR r, s, AND t?

Learn:

- Write the uppercase letters for **r**, **s**, and **t**.
- Read VCe syllables.

Vocabulary:

VCe syllable *[vē sē ē ´sǐ lŭ bŭl]* – a syllable that has one vowel letter followed by a consonant and a silent final e, and the first vowel makes its long sound

---

Listen and review.
Mark ⊠ when done.

RI

Trace and write the letters.

R R R R R

Rr Rr

Write the sentence.

1) Rex ran on a red rug.

Ss

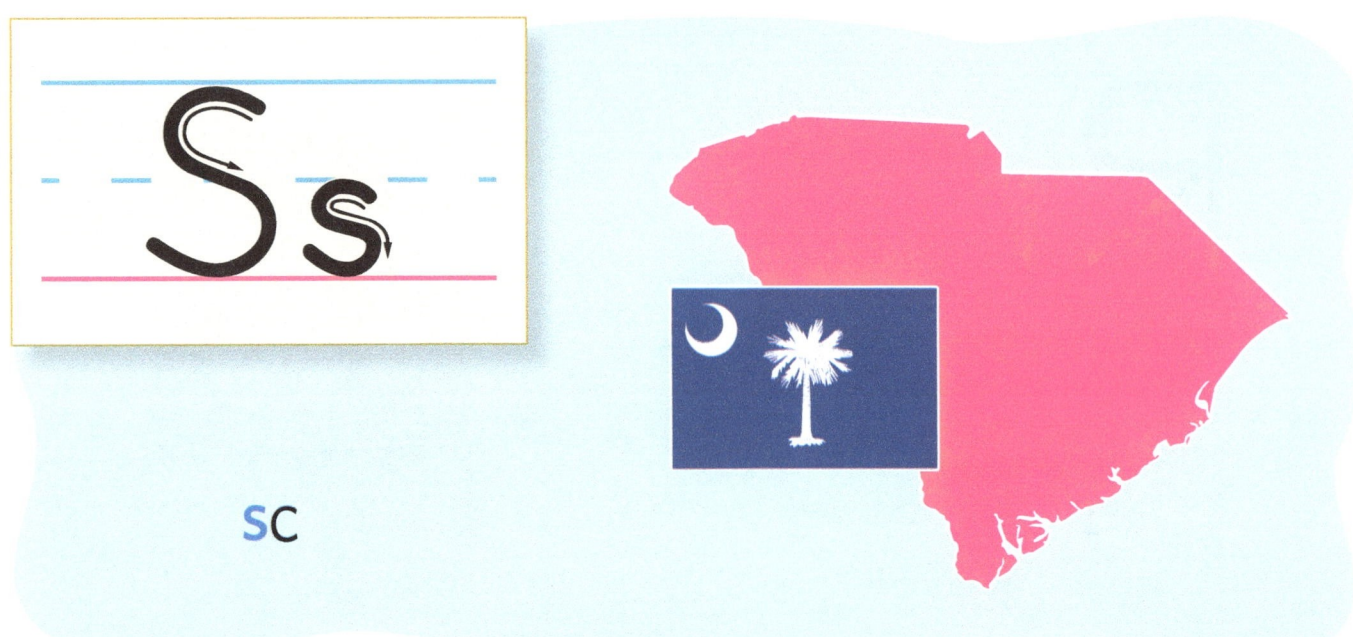

SC

Trace and write the letters.

Write the sentence.

2) Sam sent a small silk swan.

TN

Trace and write the letters.

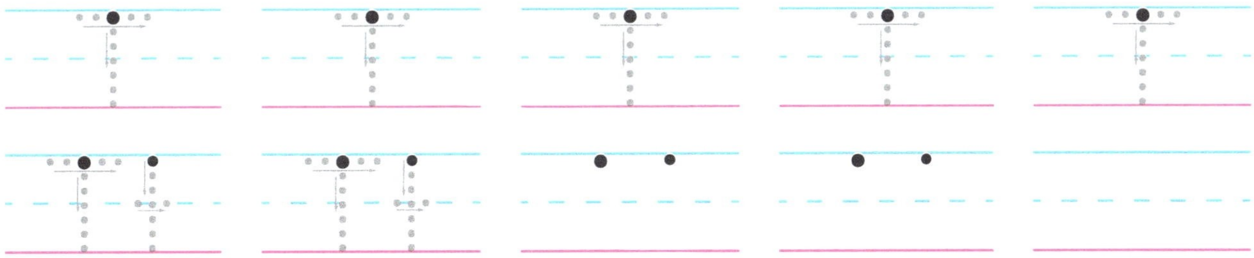

Write the sentence.

3) Tall Tom can tap a tin can.

 **Write the missing capital letters.**

4) A, B, ___, ___, ___, F, G,

___, ___, ___, J, K, ___, ___, ___,

O, P, ___, R, ___,

VCe Syllables: A **VCe syllable** has one vowel letter followed by a consonant and a silent final **e**. The vowel makes its long sound.

The arrow shows that silent final **e** makes the vowel letter long.

Read, write, and circle the correct answers.
Draw an arrow from the silent final **e** to the first vowel.

Read	Write	Circle

5) lime

lime

6) cake

7) bite

apple cat tree two

8) tape

9) rope

10) cube

WRITING PHONOGRAM REVIEW

 Listen to and write the phonograms.
Underline any multi-letter phonograms.

ACTIVITY: Everyday VCe Words

Read, trace, and write the everyday VCe words.

Read	Trace	Write
use	use	
came	came	
here	here	
home	home	
like	like	

8. WHAT ARE THE UPPERCASE LETTERS FOR u, v, AND w?

Learn:

- Write the uppercase letters for **u**, **v**, and **w**.

- Read words with the second sound of **c**.

Listen and review.
Mark ☒ when done.

WORKING WITH SOUNDS

READING PHONOGRAM REVIEW

UT

Trace and write the letters.

Write the sentence.

1) Ute will run up a hill.

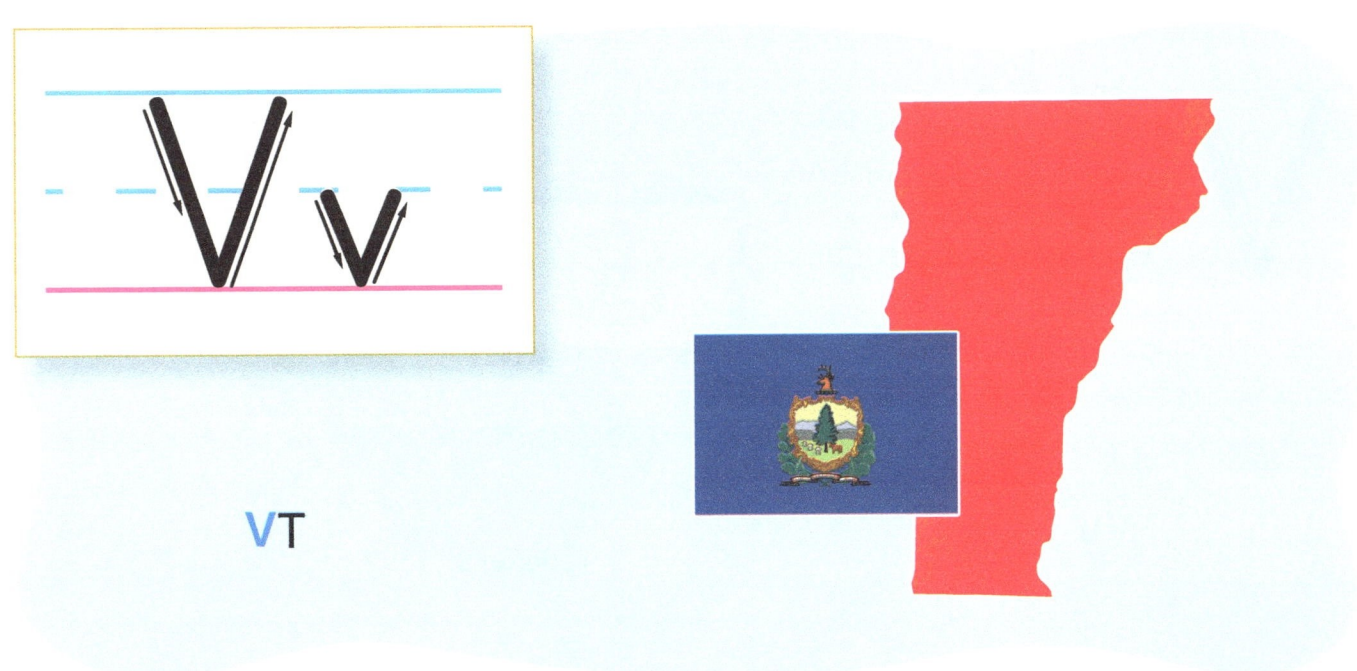

VT

Trace and write the letters.

V V V V V

v v

Write the sentence.

2) Val had a vase in a van.

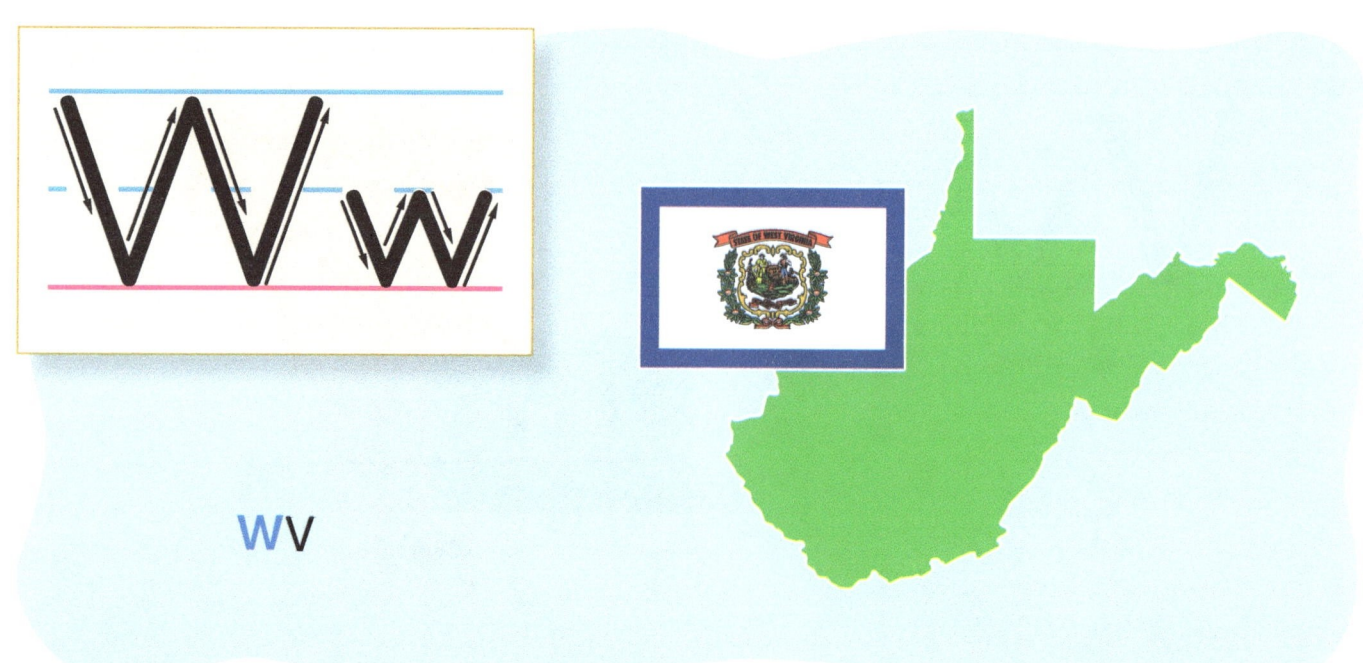

WV

 **Trace and write the letters.**

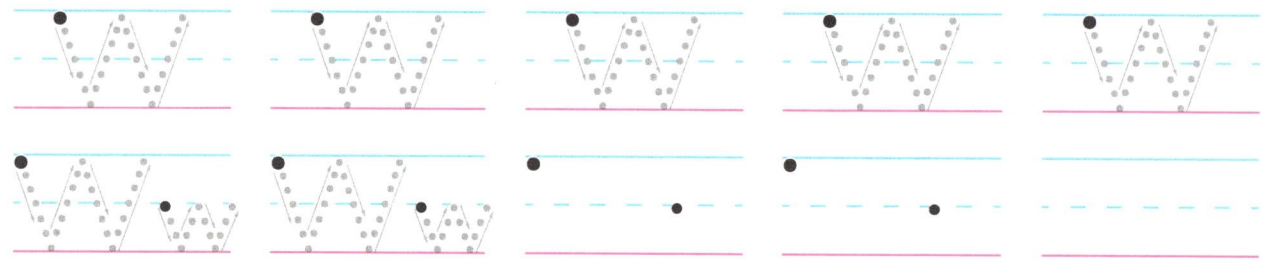

Write the sentence.

3) Wade will win a wig.

Write the missing capital letters.

4) ____, ____, C, D, E, ____, ____,

____, ____, J, K, L, ____, ____,

____, ____, Q, R, ____, ____, ____,

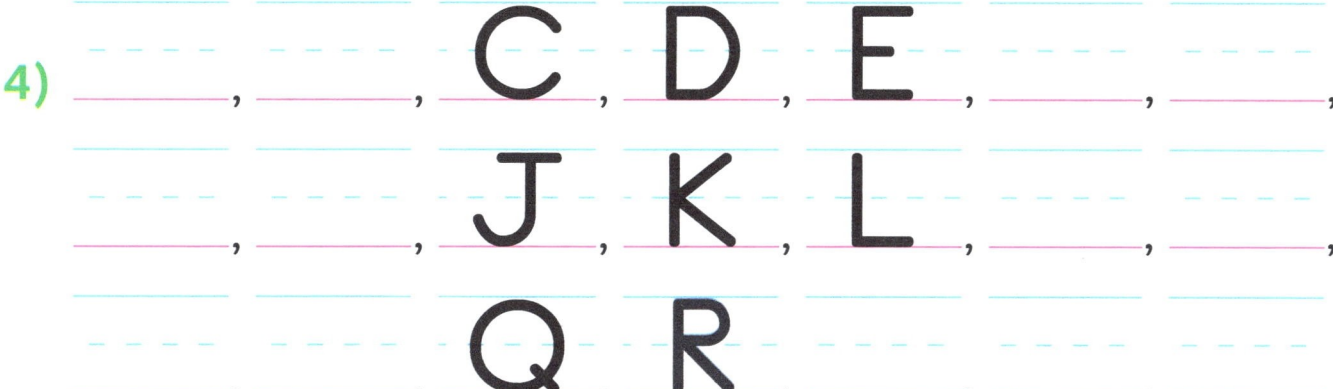

2nd Sound of **c**: Letter **c** makes its second sound before **e**, **i**, or **y**.

fan**c**y **c**ity mi**c**e

 **Fill in the blanks to complete the sentences.**

cents	ice	race

5) Vic will run in a _____.

6) He can win ten _____.

7) He will want _____ cubes in a cup.

WRITING PHONOGRAM REVIEW

✏️ **Listen to and write the phonograms.**
Underline any multi-letter phonograms.

SCORE   CORRECT   RESCORE

ACTIVITY: Reading Rules

You have learned three types of syllables. They tell you if a vowel sound will be short or long.

Closed	Open	VCe

Jill	**J**o	**J**a**ce**
short vowel	long vowel	long vowel

Read and mark ☒ the syllable type.

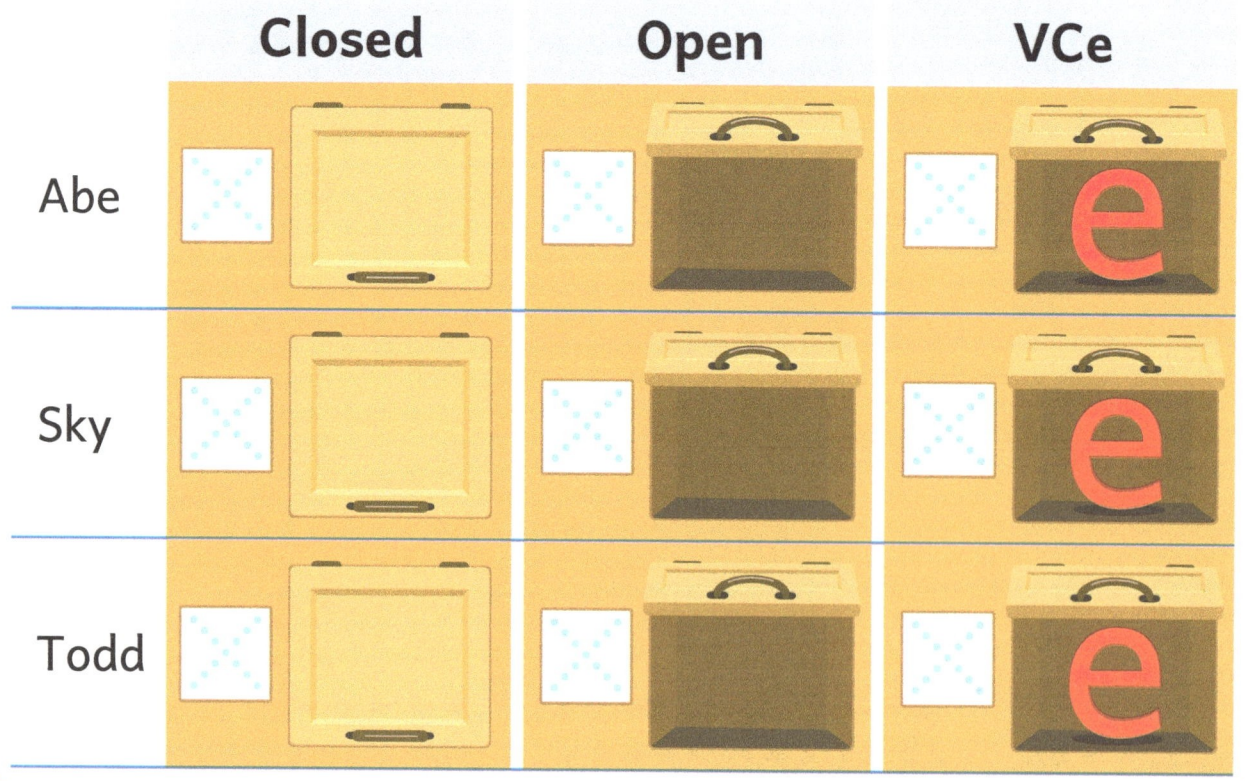

	Closed	Open	VCe
Ty			e
Blake			e
Jane			e
Meg			e
Will			e
Steve			e
Kim			e

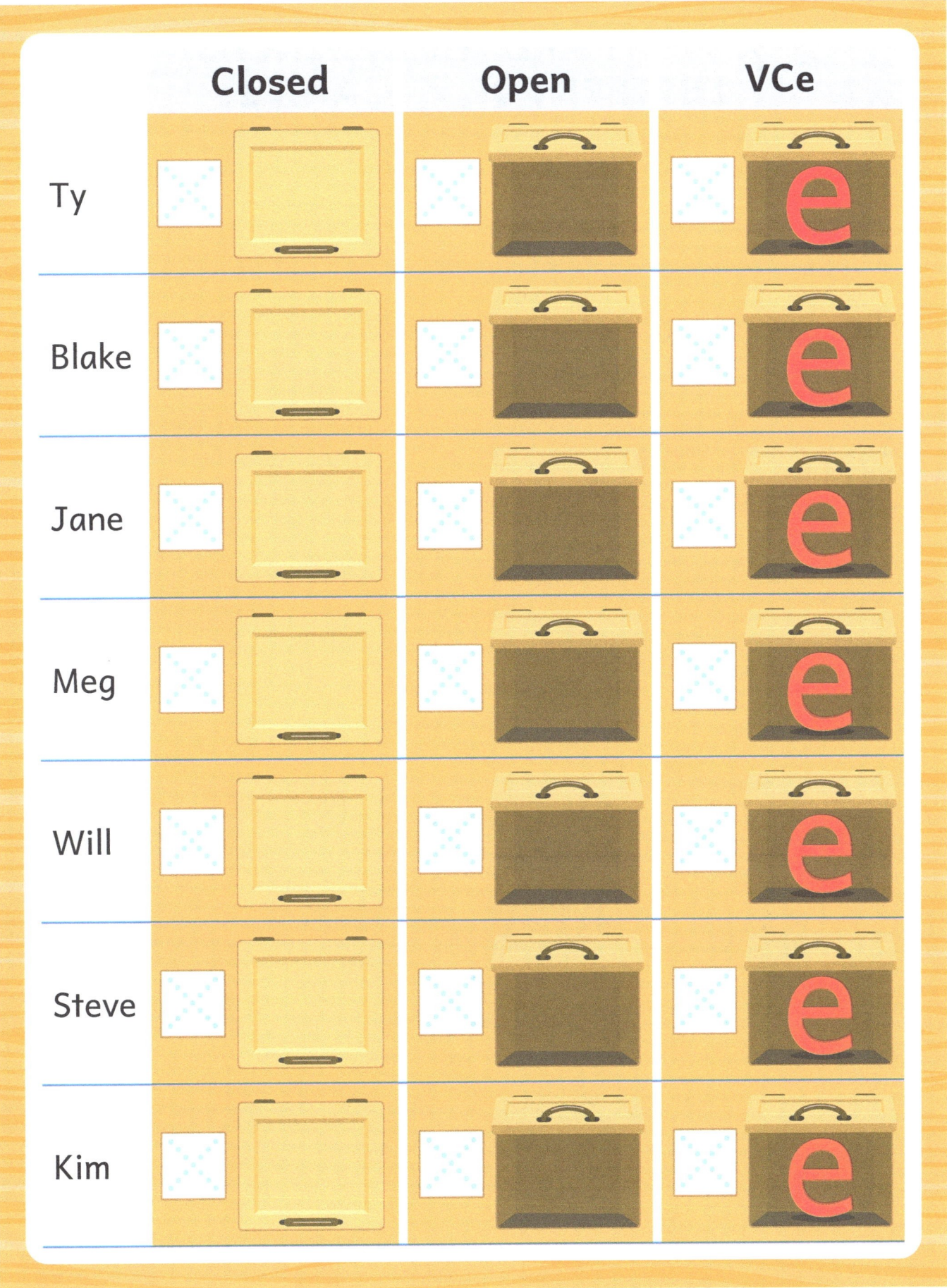

9. WHAT ARE THE UPPERCASE LETTERS FOR x, y, AND z?

Learn:

- Write the uppercase letters for **x**, **y**, and **z**.

- Read words with the second sound of **g**.

**Listen and review.
Mark ⊠ when done.**

TX

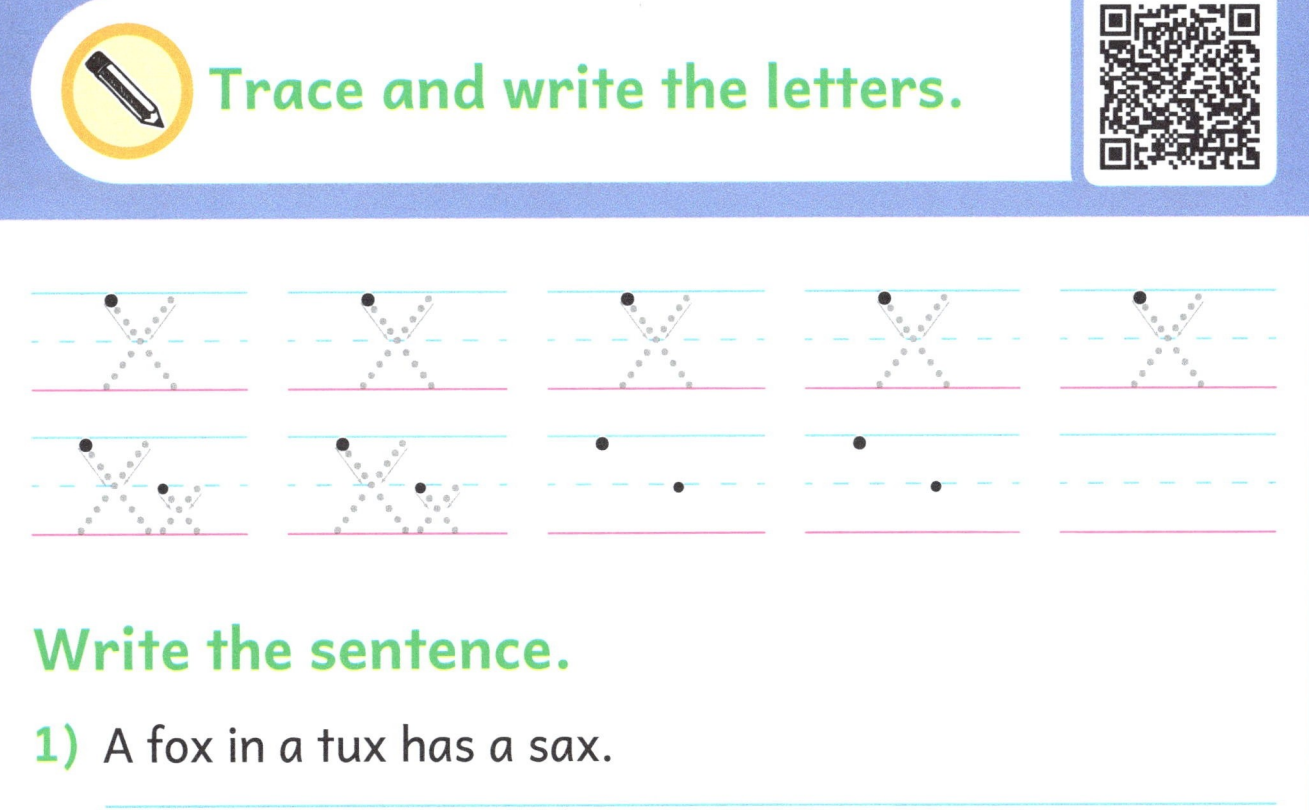

Trace and write the letters.

Write the sentence.

1) A fox in a tux has a sax.

NY

✏️ **Trace and write the letters.**

Write the sentence.

2) My yak will yelp if we yell at it.

AZ

🖊️ **Trace and write the letters.**

Z Z Z Z Z

Z z Z z

Write the sentence.

3) Zane can zig and zag in a zone.

 **Write the missing capital letters.**

4) A, ____, C, ____, E, ____, G,
____, I, ____, K, ____, M, ____,
O, ____, Q, ____, S, ____, U,
____, W, ____, Y, ____,

Reading Rules

2nd Sound of **g**: Letter **g** can make its first or second sound before **e**, **i**, or **y**. It always makes its second sound before a silent final **e**.

ge**t** hu**ge** **g**i**ft**

Circle the correct answers.
Which picture describes the sentence?

5) Zac put his pet in a cage.

6) A man went on stage to tell a joke.

7) I put my name on a page.

WRITING PHONOGRAM REVIEW

✏️ **Listen to and write the phonograms.**
Underline any multi-letter phonograms.

SCORE   CORRECT   RESCORE

PHONOGRAM REVIEW

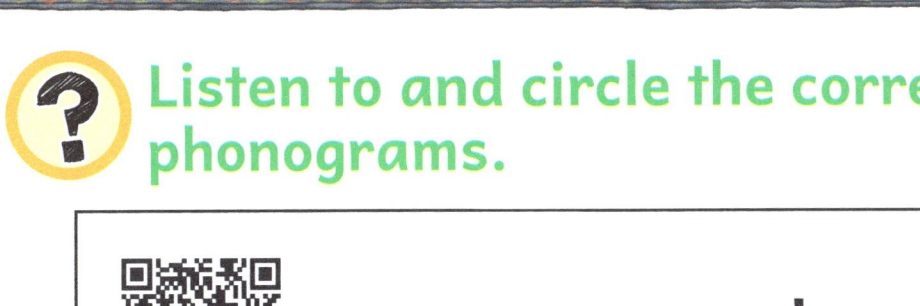

? Listen to and circle the correct phonograms.

1) t   h   w

2) w   o   u

3) l   t   f

4) c   k   s

5) qu   j   p

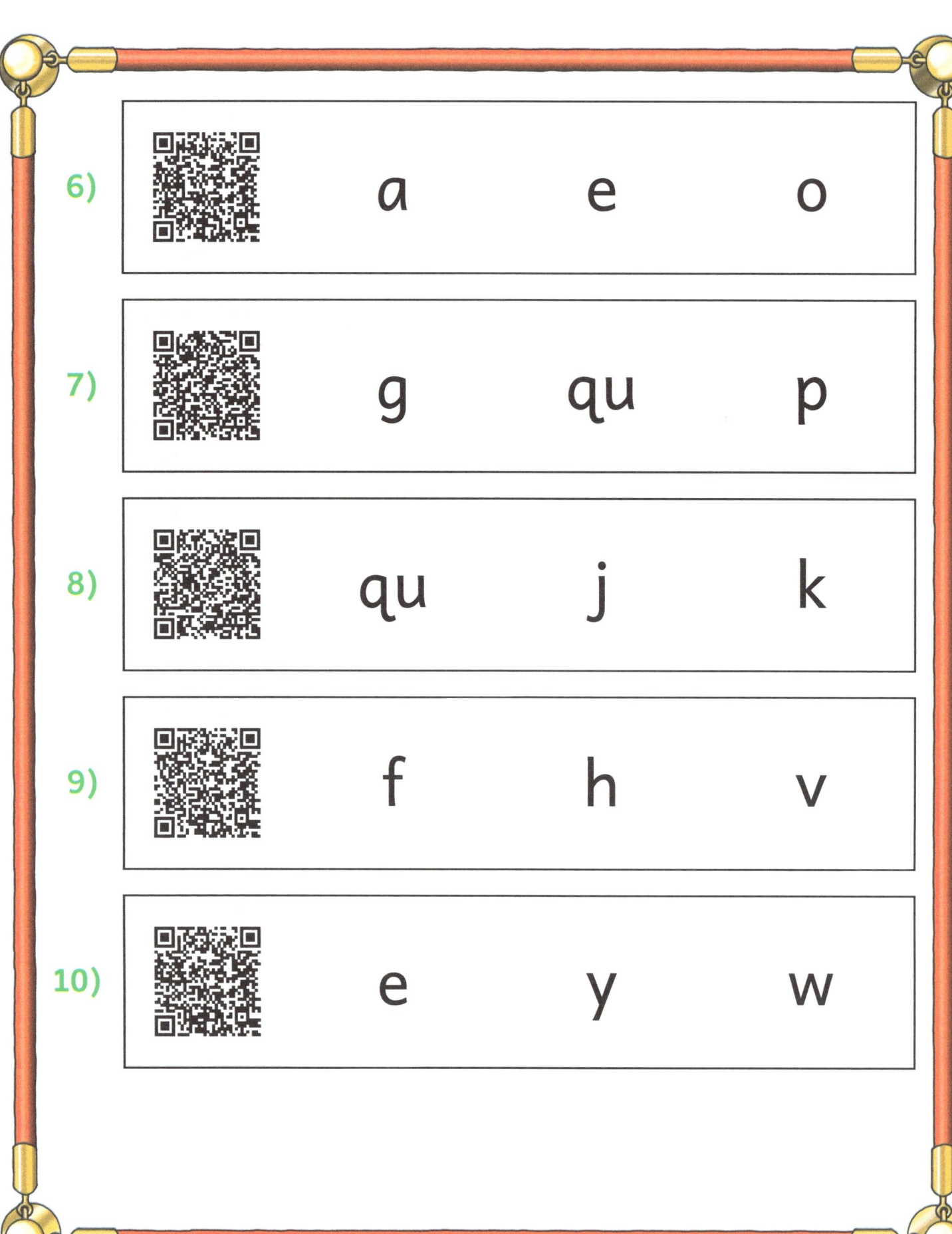

6)   a   e   o

7)   g   qu   p

8)   qu   j   k

9)   f   h   v

10)   e   y   w

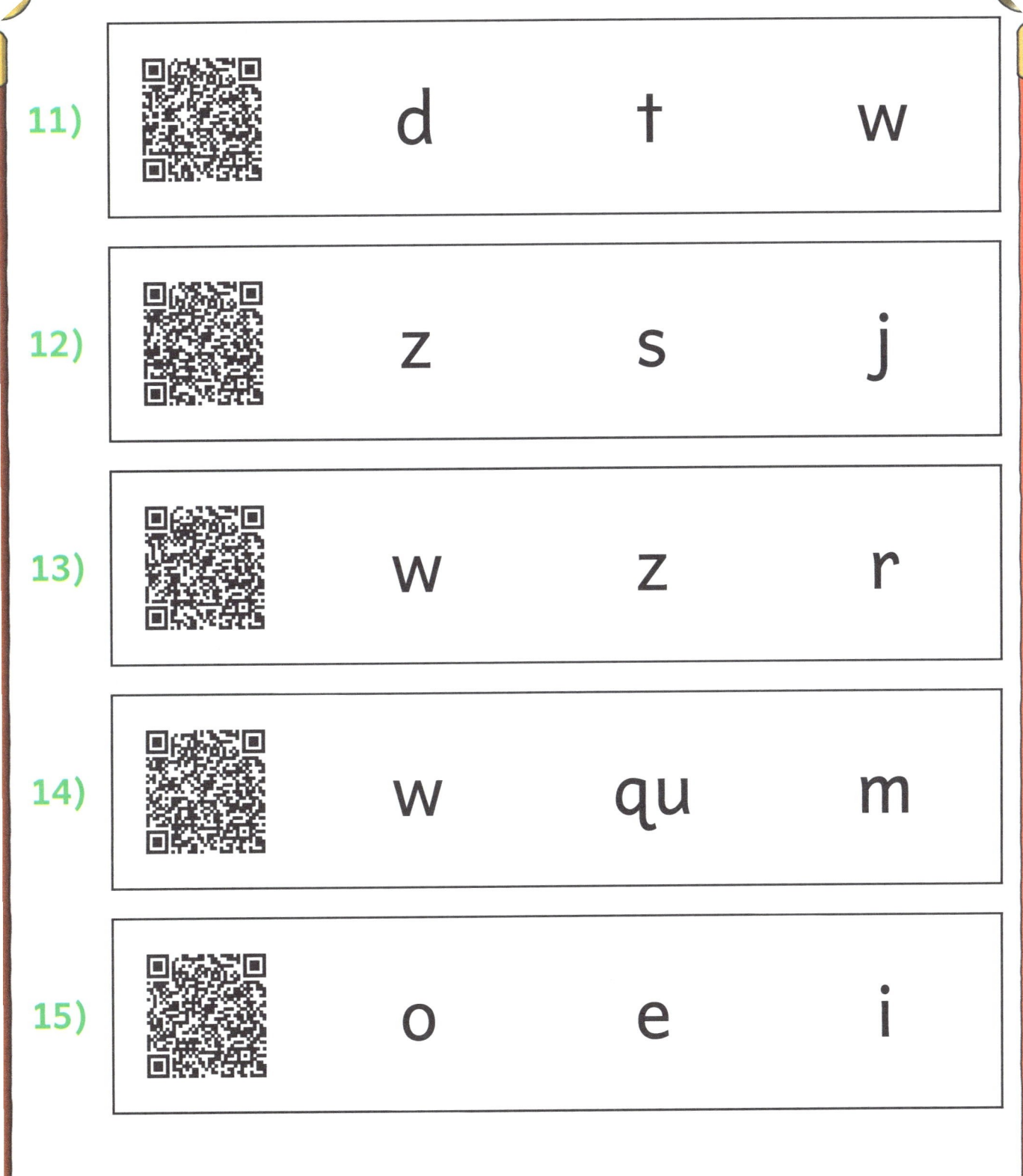

11)   d   t   w

12)   z   s   j

13)   w   z   r

14)   w   qu   m

15)   o   e   i

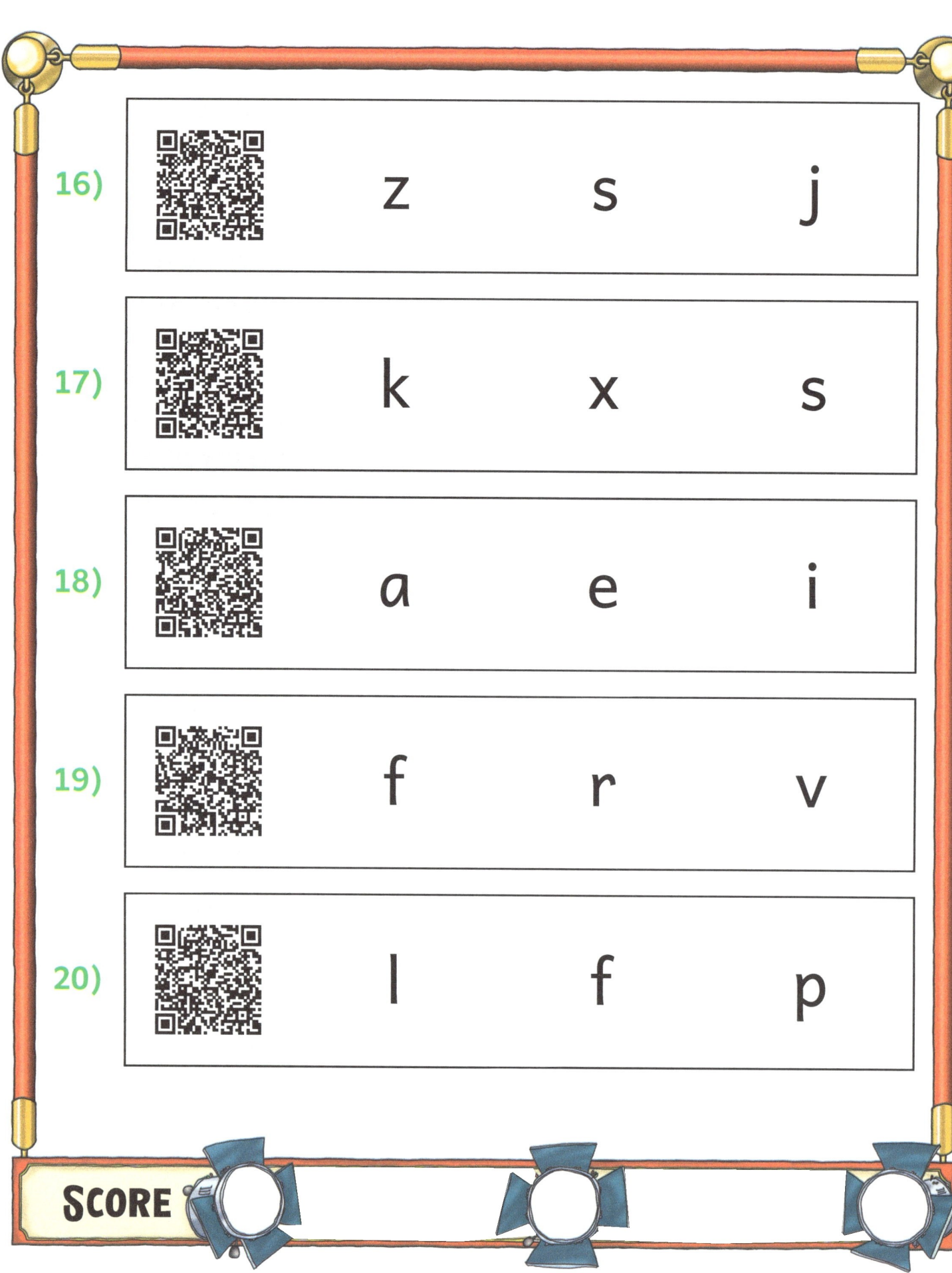

16) z   s   j

17) k   x   s

18) a   e   i

19) f   r   v

20) l   f   p

SCORE

READER 1: "We Go in a Jet"

Practice these everyday words.

	Read	Trace			Read	Trace
1)	we	we	6)		but	but
2)	in	in	7)		is	is
3)	a	a	8)		and	and
4)	on	on	9)		has	has
5)	can	can	10)		at	at

Time to Read!

Reader I

We Go in a Jet

 **Choose the correct answers.**

11) Where are the characters?
- ○ on a farm
- ○ on a beach
- ○ in a forest

12) How did the characters get there?
- ○ in a jet
- ○ in a car
- ○ in a boat

13) Why is Pip mad and sad?
- ○ He is wet.
- ○ He is tired.
- ○ He is hot.

14) Do the words *milk* and *flat* begin with the same sound?
- ○ Yes
- ○ No

Phonogram Test 6

Listen to and write the correct phonograms.
Underline any multi-letter phonograms.

1)

2)

3)

4)

5)

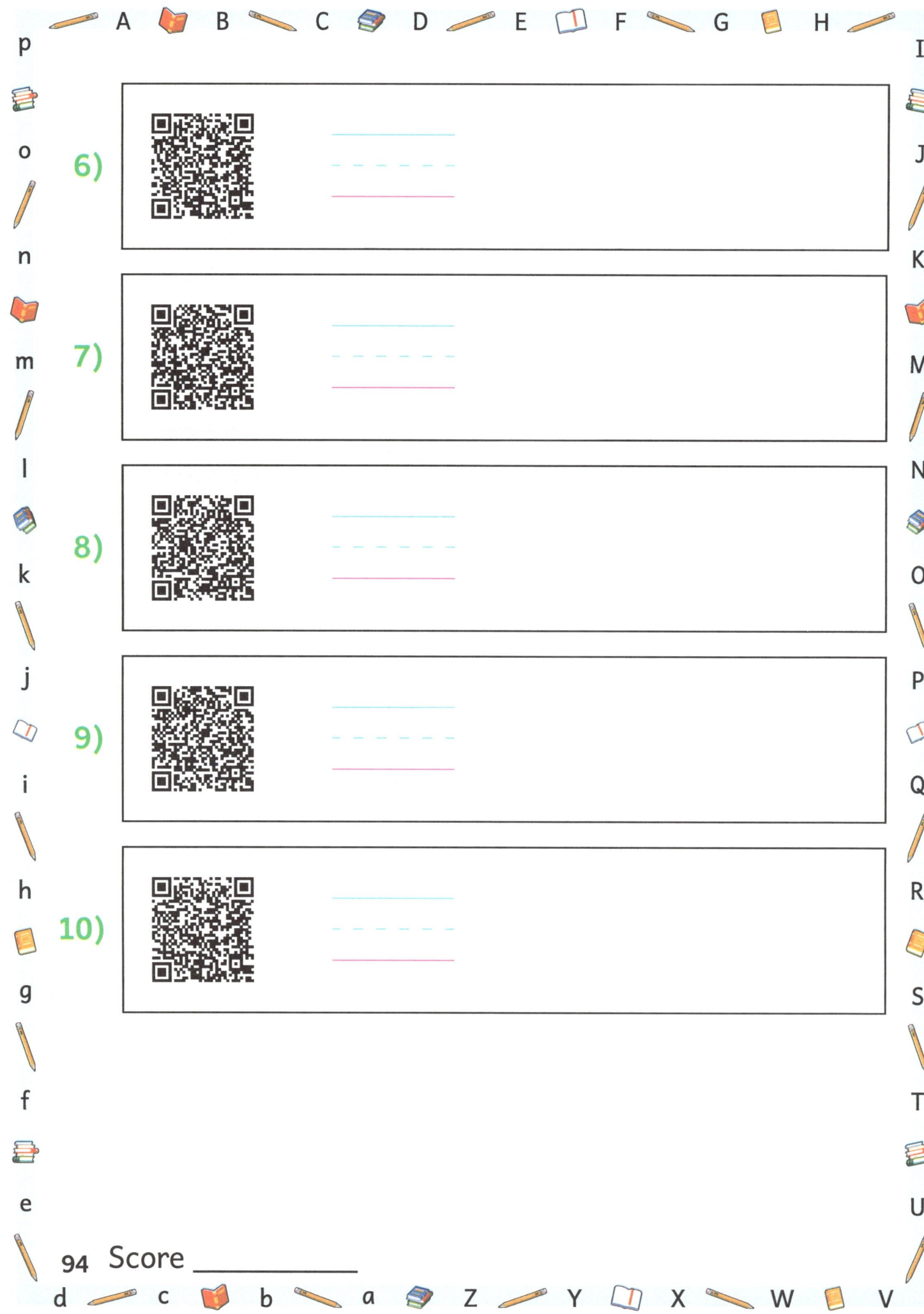

Score _____